What Others Are Saying About This Book:

No matter what writing program you're teaching, this book is a must-have in the classroom.

—Anna Goble, Fourth Grade Teacher

This book is a great tool for students and classroom teachers alike. All of the writing supports we piece together can now be found in one resource.

—Jean Southland, Sixth Grade Teacher

Writing is a difficult subject to teach and learn. Writing well is even more challenging. **Young Writers' Toolkit** *is a user-friendly tool for both teacher and student. It provides clear choices to help students improve the quality of their writing and to help teachers teach writing to their students. This is an excellent resource that every school should have.*

—PJ Foehr, Principal

I love writing and I use this book to help me all the time.

—Tyler Sadoff, student and budding author

Young Writers' Toolkit

Michael C. Fine

Veronica Hoyle-Kent

First Edition

Per Se Press, Morgan Hill, California

Young Writers' Toolkit

Michael C. Fine
Veronica Hoyle-Kent

Published by:
Per Se Press
1487 Santa Ines Way
Morgan Hill, CA 95037, U.S.A.
info@persepress.com
http://www.persepress.com

Library of Congress Control Number: 2009922330

ISBN 978-0-9823306-2-3 (paperback)

Edited by Jordan Rosenfeld (jordansmuse@gmail.com)
Cover design by Marieke Ruys (mariekeruys@yahoo.com)

Printed in the United States of America

10 9 8 7 6 5 4 3 2 1

Contents

About The Authors

Mike Fine is the co-creator of Young Writers' Story Deck Writing Program. He writes technical, marketing, and educational pieces for high tech companies and school districts. He has written novels, short stories, screen plays and stage plays. Mike is an active volunteer in the Morgan Hill Unified School District and at Rocketship Education in San Jose, California.

Veronica Hoyle-Kent is the co-creator of Young Writers' Story Deck Writing Program. She is the mother of two and a dedicated volunteer in the Morgan Hill Unified School District. She writes children's stories and has worked with young writers in the classroom for many years.

Foreword

Writing well is hard. Teaching students to write well is perhaps even harder. We wrote this book to help make things easier for students and teachers alike. We sincerely hope that students around the world are able to write better, in less time, and with less stress and frustration by using this book.

If you have any suggestions on how to improve this book, please let us know. You may send email to:

info@persepress.com

Acknowledgements

We would like to thank:

The teachers at Nordstrom Elementary School, who have inspired our children to write, and inspired us to create this book.

Anna Goble, Jean Southland, Carol Sheets, Greenwell Seger, Randall Seger, Monique Sadoff, Tyler Sadoff, Jane Hopwood, Lauren Welch, Greg Claytor, Doris Barrow, Fern Fine, and PJ Foehr for their assistance reviewing and improving this book.

Volunteers Cassiopeia Bates, Kathleen Hanlon, Lisa Kaminsky, Kristen Judy Tatroe, and Maria Nguyen for their early contributions to the "better word" portion of this book.

Brad and Cinda at BookSmart, who graciously filled us up with soda and tea as we wrote large portions of this book at their book store.

The happy crew at the Starbuck's on Walnut Grove Drive in Morgan Hill, who allowed us to commandeer a table there, too.

Anyone else who contributed to the content, editing, and design of this book. We apologize if we've omitted you!

A Word from the Authors

We've watched hundreds of students struggle to write well. We've watched dozens of teachers struggle to teach their students to write well. And we think we've written a book that will help students and teachers alike.

Good writing doesn't just happen but is forged, like a glorious skyscraper out of a puddle of molten steel. Good writing is a possibility for every student, with the right tools. This book contains these tools:

Word Lists: Sometimes writing well means finding just the right word to describe someone or something. We've got a rich collection of word lists to help.

Word Groups: Sometimes writing well means immersing yourself in the lingo of a particular world, time, or subject. We've got a treasury of word groups ranging from ancient civilizations to the old west to the vastness of space.

Better Words: Sometimes writing well means replacing plain, boring, overused words with better choices. We've got a list of these "jail words" and lists of better, "get out of jail" replacement words.

Weak Words: Sometimes writing well means removing unnecessary, redundant, and weak words that clutter and slow your writing. We've got a list of these weak words and guidelines on how to remove or replace them.

Other Resources: We've also included commonly misspelled words, commonly misused words, how to cite sources, onomatopoeia words, story elements, how to use quotation marks, dialogue tags, sentence starters, and proofreading marks.

We hope students around the world write better by using this book. And remember...Write today. Write tomorrow. Write every day!

Michael C. Fine
Veronica Hoyle-Kent
Morgan Hill, California
Summer 2009

Disclaimer

Every effort has been made to ensure that this book is as complete and as accurate as possible. However, there may be mistakes both typographical and in content.

The purpose of this manual is to educate and entertain. The authors and Per Se Press shall have neither liability nor responsibility to any person or entity with respect to any loss or damage caused or alleged to be caused directly or indirectly by the information contained in this book.

If you do not wish to be bound by the above, you may return this book to the publisher for a full refund.

About this Book

For your convenience, this book is bound with a lay-flat binding. To make the book lie flat, turn to the desired page and press gently in the middle of the book.

The body text of this book is typeset with Century Schoolbook. Headings are set with Antique Olive Black.

Part I: Word Lists

In this section you'll find an organized collection of descriptive words which you can often use to improve your sentences. Use the words on these word lists when you are describing people, places, and things.

Example:

Needs Editing:	**Better:**
Anne stared into the eyes of the creature.	Anne stared into the <u>enormous</u> creature's <u>wild</u>, <u>bloodshot</u> eyes.

In this example, the underlined words were found on the "describing characters—eyes" and "size" word lists.

Use the whitespace on the bottom of the pages to add your own words when you think of them (unless you are using a shared classroom book or your teacher has told you not to write in your book).

Word Lists

senses—touch

boiling
breezy
brittle
broken
bumpy
chilly
coarse
cold
cool
cracked
crisp
crooked
crunchy
crusty
cuddly
curly
damp
dirty
dry
dusty
elastic
filthy
fine
firm
flaky
fleshy
fluffy
fragile
frosty
frozen
furry
fuzzy
greasy
gritty
hard
heavy
hollow
hot
humid
icy
jagged
knotty
leathery
loose
lukewarm
lumpy
mushy
oily
painful
plastic
pointy
prickly
pulpy
rainy
rickety
rough
rubbery
sandy
satiny
scratchy
shaggy
shaky
sharp

(continued on next page)

senses—touch *(continued)*

shivering
silky
slick
slimy
slippery
slushy
smooth
soft
soggy
solid
spongy
steady
steamy
sticky
stiff
tender
tepid
thick
thin
tight
uneven
velvety
viscous
warm
waxy
weak
wet
wobbly
wooden
wooly
wrinkled

senses—sound

babbling
barking
bashing
bawling
baying
beating
bellowing
blasting
bleating
booming
braying
bubbling
buzzing
cackling
cawing
chanting
chattering
chiming
chirping
clanking
clashing
clattering
clicking
clinking
cooing
cracking
crackling
crashing
creaking
croaking
crowing
crying
deafening
distinct
droning
drumming
ear-piercing
faint
fizzing
fizzling
flapping
gleeful
grating
groaning
growling
grumbling
grunting
gurgling
harsh
haunting
high-pitched
hissing
hooting
howling
humming
hushed
husky
irritating
jingling
laughing
loud
melodic
meowing
mewing
moaning
mumbling
murmuring
muted
muttering
neighing
noisy
pealing
peeping
popping
puffing
purring
quacking
quiet

(continued on next page)

senses—sound *(continued)*

raspy
resonant
ringing
ripping
roaring
rumbling
rustling
screaming
screeching
shattering
shrieking
shrill
silent
sizzling
slurping
smacking
smashing
snapping
snarling
snoring
snorting
soft
sorrowful
splashing
squalling
squeaking
squealing
squishing
thrumming
thudding
thumping
thundering
ticking
tinkling
tooting
twanging
twittering
wailing
warbling
wheezing
whining
whirring
whispering
whistling
yapping
yelling
yelping
zapping
zipping

senses—smell

acrid
aromatic
briny
burnt
earthy
fishy
floral
fragrant
fresh
fruity
grassy
heady
mild
mildewy
moldy
musty
odorous
perfumed
piney
pungent
putrid
rancid
reeking
ripe
rotten
savory
scented
sharp
sickly
sour
spicy
spoiled
stale
stinky
strong
sweet
tempting

senses—taste

bitter
bittersweet
bland
burnt
buttery
crisp
delicious
fishy
fresh
fruity
gingery
hot
juicy
luscious
medicinal
mellow
mild
oily
overripe
peppery
plain
pulpy
raw
ripe
rotten
salty
savory
sour
spicy
spoiled
strong
sugary
sweet
tangy
tart
tasteless
tasty
unripe
vinegary

shape

angular
arched
blunt
boxy
branching
broad
broken
chubby
chunky
circular
concave
convex
crimped
crinkled
crooked
curved
deep
domed
fat
flared
flat
frilled
hexagonal
hollow
irregular
jutting
lumpy
narrow
octagonal
oval
portly
pyramidical
rectangular
rolled
rotund
round
ruffled
scalloped
shallow
shapeless
shapely
skinny
spindly
split
square
steep
straight
swollen
tapering
thick
top-heavy
triangular
twiggy
wavy
wide
winged
wiry
wrinkled

size

average
big
colossal
enormous
fat
giant
gigantic
great
huge
immense
large
little
long
mammoth
massive
medium
middle-sized
miniature
petite
pudgy
puny
runty
scant
short
small
stocky
tall
thin
tiny
wee

time

afternoon
ancient
autumn (fall)
blink
brief
brisk
century
continual
crawling
daily
dawn
daybreak
decade
dusk
early
era
eternity
evening
fast
flash
fortnight
hour
instant
intermittent
late
lengthy
long
mid-morning
midnight
minute
modern
moment
monthly
month
morning
nanosecond
night
noon
old
old-fashioned
outdated
period
periodic
punctual
quick
rapid
second
short
slow
sporadic
spring
summer
swift
tardy
twilight
weekly
week
witching-hour
winter
yearly
year
young

quantity

abundant
ample
bit
bunch
bushel
countless
couple
dozen
dribble
drop
drop in the bucket
empty
few
full
great
handful
heavy
infinite
iota
light
limited
many
meager
multitude
myriad
numerous
overflowing
portion
scant
scattering
several
single
slew
smattering
smidgen
some
sprinkling
ton
trifle
unlimited
vast

color—red

blood red
brick
burgundy
cardinal
carmine
cherry
claret
coral
cranberry
crimson
flame
garnet
henna
lobster
magenta
maroon
rose
rouge
ruby
ruddy
rust
sanguine
scarlet
strawberry
titian
tomato
vermilion
wine

color—pink

blush
bubblegum
carnation
coral
cotton candy
rose
salmon

color—yellow

butter
buttercup
butterscotch
canary
daffodil
flax
gilded
gold
golden
lemon
mustard
saffron
sallow
sandy
straw
sunny
tawny
topaz

color—orange

apricot
brass
carrot
copper
peach
pumpkin
shrimp
tangerine

color—blue

aqua
aquamarine
azure
cerulean
cobalt
cornflower
electric blue
ice blue
indigo
midnight blue
navy
peacock
periwinkle
powder blue
robin's-egg
royal blue
sapphire
sky blue
steel
teal
turquoise
violet

color—purple

amethyst
heliotrope
lavender
lilac
magenta
mauve
orchid
pansy
periwinkle
plum
puce
violet
wine

color—green

apple
aquamarine
avocado
celery
chartreuse
emerald
evergreen
forest
grass
jade
kelly green
leek
lime
mint
moss
olive
pea
pine
sage
sea green
teal

color—brown

almond
amber
auburn
beige
bronze
burnt sienna
chestnut
chocolate
cinnamon
cocoa
coffee
copper
dun
fawn
ginger
hazel
henna
mahogany
nut
nutmeg
russet
rust
sandy
tan
tawny
teak
terracotta
umber
walnut

color—gray

ash
dove
dust
iron
leaden
metallic
oyster
platinum
putty
silver
slate
smoke
steel
stone

color—metallic

brass
bronze
chrome
copper
gold
pewter
platinum
rust
silver

color—white

alabaster
ashen
blanched
bleached
blonde
bone
chalk
cream
eggshell
fair
ivory
lily white
marble
milky
oyster
pearl
snow
swan

color—black

charcoal
coal
dusky
ebony
ink
jet black
licorice
midnight
obsidian
onyx
pitch
raven
sable
tar

feelings—positive

agreeable
amused
astonished
attentive
bold
brave
breezy
calm
charming
cheerful
comfortable
comforted
compassionate
considerate
content
cooperative
courageous
curious
delighted
determined
eager
elated
empowered
enchanted
enchanting
energetic
energized
enthusiastic
excited
exuberant
fair
faithful
fearless
fine
fortunate
friendly
funny
generous
gentle
gleeful
glorious
good
grateful
happy
healthy
heroic
hilarious
hopeful
invigorated
jolly
joyful
joyous
kind
lively
loving
loyal
lucky
magnificent
merry
obedient
overjoyed
passionate
patient
peaceful
peppy
perfect
perky
pleasant
relieved
rested
satisfied
serene
sheepish
silly
splendid
strong
successful
thoughtful
victorious
vivacious
witty
zealous

feelings—negative

afraid
angry
annoyed
anxious
apprehensive
ashamed
astonished
awful
awkward
bad
bored
conceited
creepy
cruel
deceitful
deceived
defeated
defiant
deflated
dejected
depressed
desperate
disgusted
disturbed
dizzy
doubtful
dreadful
eerie
embarrassed
emotional
empty
envious
evil
exhausted
faint
fearful
fierce
foggy
foolish
frantic
frightened
furious
greedy
grieving
grim
hesitant
hopeless
horrible
horrid
hungry
hurt
hysterical
ill
impatient
insistent
lazy
lonely

(continued on next page)

feelings—negative *(continued)*

mean
moody
mysterious
naughty
nervous
outraged
outrageous
pained
painful
panicky
regretful
reluctant
repulsed
repulsive
resigned
ridiculous
sad
scared
scornful
selfish
sore
sorrowful
stubborn
suspicious
tense
terrified
thoughtless
tired
troubled
uneasy
unhappy
unhealthy
upset
uptight
weak
weary
worried

describing characters—hair
(see also colors)

auburn
balding
black
bleached
blond/blonde
bouncy
braided
brittle
brown
clean
coarse
curly
damaged
damp
dirty
dry
dyed
fine
flaky
flat
fluffy
frizzy
glossy
golden
gray
healthy
highlighted
kinky
knotted
long
oily
patchy
permed
receding
red
rusty
salt and pepper
sandy blond
shaggy
shimmering
shiny
short
shoulder-length
silver
smooth
soft
spiked
straight
teased
thick
thin
tousled
wavy
white
wild
wind-blown
wiry
wispy

describing characters—ears

cauliflower
ever-listening
flapping
hairy
hidden
huge
large
long
medium
missing
pierced
pointed
pointy
red
small
sticking out

describing characters—eyes
(see also colors)

alert
almond
animated
black
blazing
bloodshot
blue
bright
brown
clear
crinkled
cunning
dark
dazed
dazzling
dreamy
droopy
dry
dull
empty
fiery
flashing
glaring
glassy
glazed
gleaming
glowering
glowing
green
hazel
hooded
iridescent
lazy
luminous
menacing
narrowed
piercing
puffy
round
scowling
shining
sinister
slanted
sleepy
small
sorrowful
soulless
sparkling
speckled
squinty
sunken
swollen
tearful
twinkling
twitchy
watery
wide
wide-set
wild

describing characters—mouth/lips

cupid's bow
drooling
droopy
dry
fat
frowning
full
perfectly-formed
pouty
puckered
puffy
pursed
quivering
small
smiling
snarling
stretched
thin
tight
trembling
turned down
turned up
twitching
wet
wide

describing characters—teeth

bright
broken
buck-toothed
capped
chipped
clenched
crooked
dingy
even
gritted
gritty
jagged
loose
missing
pearly-white
perfect
rotted
stained
straight
yellow

describing characters—nose

bloody
bony
broken
bulbous
bumpy
button
congested
crooked
dripping
flaring nostrils
hawkish
hooked
large
long
narrow
pierced
pointy
prominent
pug
roman
runny
snotty
straight
upturned
warty

describing characters—skin

alabaster
ashen
black
blotchy
brown
bruised
burned
burnt
clean
clear
dark
dirty
drab
dry
ebony
fair
flaky
flushed
freckled
fresh
golden
grimy
ivory
leathery
milky
muddy
olive
pale
pasty
peeling
pimply
pink
radiant
red
rosy
rough
scarred
scraped
scrubbed
silky
smooth
soft
spotty
stretched
sun-burnt
sun-kissed
tan
tattooed
translucent
weathered
white
worn
wrinkled
yellow
young

describing characters—body

beefy
big
bony
brawny
bulky
burly
chubby
curvaceous
emaciated
enormous
erect
fat
fleshy
gaunt
gigantic
hardy
heavy
huge
husky
immense
lanky
large
lean
lumbering
massive
muscular
obese
plump
portly
robust
rotund
scrawny
short
shriveled
skeletal
skinny
slender
slight
small
statuesque
stout
strong
sturdy
swollen
tall
thick
thin
tiny
towering
unwieldy
wide
wispy

describing characters—appearance

adorable
alert
animated
attractive
beautiful
blushing
bright
captivating
clean
clownish
colorful
cuddly
cute
dainty
dangerous
dirty
disheveled
dowdy
drab
dreadful
elegant
exhausted
exotic
expensive
flashy
fragile
frail
gaudy
gentle
glamorous
gorgeous
graceful
grim
gross
grotesque
handsome
harsh
healthy
hideous
homely
kindly
lively
lovely
meek
messy
pleasant
poised
poor
radiant
regal
rough
scruffy
shabby
showy
sickly
sloppy
slovenly
soft
splendid
stern
stumbling
stunning
tidy
tired
ugly
ungraceful
untidy
wealthy

describing characters—personality/behavior

admirable
agreeable
amiable
arrogant
attentive
blunt
boastful
bold
brainy
bratty
brave
bright
brilliant
calm
carefree
careful
cautious
charitable
charming
cheery
childish
clever
clownish
clumsy
competitive
conceited
confident
considerate
cordial
corrupt
courageous
courteous
crafty
creative
crude
cultured
cunning
curious
dangerous
deceitful
delightful
demanding
despicable
devilish
difficult
dishonorable
disorderly
disrespectful
distant
disturbed
dopey
dorky
dramatic
dull
dumb
easy-going
eccentric
ecstatic
educated
elated
energetic
engaging
evil
extroverted
faithful
fearless
fiendish
forgiving
formidable
friendly
frosty
funny

(continued on next page)

describing characters—personality/behavior *(continued)*

geeky
generous
genial
gentle
giving
gloating
good
good-natured
goofy
gracious
greedy
guarded
gutsy
happy
harsh
haughty
heartless
helpful
heroic
hilarious
honest
honorable
humble
icy
ignorant
ill-tempered
impatient
impolite
indecent
indulgent
insane
insecure
intoxicated
intriguing
introverted
intuitive
irrational
irresistible
jealous
joyful
just
kind
kind-hearted
lazy
liar
lighthearted
likeable
lively
loud
loving
loyal
lucky
malicious
mean
meddling
mischievous
miserly
modest
monstrous
murderous
nerdy
nice
noisy
nosy
nurturing
obedient
obnoxious
overjoyed
paranoid
pathetic
patient
persistent
persuasive
perverse
pious
pleasant
pleased
polite
popular
precocious
quiet

(continued on next page)

describing characters—personality/behavior *(continued)*

reasonable
rebellious
refined
remarkable
respectful
responsible
righteous
rigid
rotten
rowdy
rude
sane
savage
scheming
scholarly
selfish
selfless
sensitive
serious
severe
shameful
shameless
shrewd
shy
sinister
sly
smart
snooty
snotty
soft-spoken
solitary
sour
spirited
spoiled
stern
stingy
strange
strict
stubborn
stuck-up
stupid
successful
sunny
suspicious
sweet
tactful
talented
thoughtful
thoughtless
tight-fisted
timid
tolerant
transparent
troubled
trusting
truthful
uncultured
uneducated
unique
unlucky
unpolished
unpopular
unreasonable
untroubled
vicious
vile
violent
vivacious
vulgar
well-meaning
wicked
wild
wily
wise
zealous

describing places/scene
(see also smell, touch, sound)

abandoned
airy
ancient
arid
average
balmy
barren
beautiful
blustery
breezy
bright
brilliant
calm
cavernous
charming
chilly
clean
clear
cloudy
cold
comfortable
cool
cozy
creepy
crowded
cute
damp
dank
dark
decrepit
deep
desolate
dilapidated
dim
dirty
disgusting
disreputable
distant
drafty
dreary
dull
dumpy
dusty
elegant
empty
enchanting
exotic
fair
fancy
far
fashionable
filthy
flat
flooded
foggy
forbidding
foreboding
fresh
glamorous
glittering
glorious
grassy
grim
grimy
gusty
haunted
hazy
hideous
high
hilly
homey
horrid
hot
humid
icy
immaculate
infested
light

(continued on next page)

describing places/scene *(continued)*
(see also smell, touch, sound)

loud
low
luminous
mediocre
mild
mildewed
misty
modern
modest
moldy
moonlit
mountainous
muddy
murky
musty
noisy
old-fashioned
overcast
picturesque
plain
polluted
private
quaint
quiet
rainy
rickety
rundown
sandy
scorched
shabby
shadowy
silent
slimy
slippery
slushy
smelly
smoggy
smoky
snowy
spacious
special
spotless
stark
steamy
sticky
still
stinky
stormy
strange
stunning
suitable
summery
sun-baked
sun-drenched
sunlit
sunny
temperate
thundering
tidy
towering
trendy
tropical
underground
unsightly
unusual
vast
warm
well-lit
wet
whimsical
wide
wide-open
windswept
windy
wooded

Part II: Word Groups

In this section you'll find a collection of what we call "word groups." If you ever need to immerse yourself in the lingo of a particular world, time, or subject, use the appropriate list(s) here. Some of these words you'll already know, some may be new to you. Hopefully all of them will put you in the mood to write a great story.

Use the whitespace on the bottom of the pages to add your own words when you think of them (unless you are using a shared classroom book or your teacher has told you not to write in your book).

Word Groups

Fantasy / Magic

banshee	A spirit in the form of a wailing woman who appears as an omen that a family member will soon die.
bewitch	To place under one's power by or as if by magic; cast a spell upon.
brownie	A small sprite thought to do helpful work at night.
cast	To send forth as in "cast a spell."
castle	A fortified residence, as of a prince or noble.
centaur	A creature having the head, trunk, and arms of a man, and the body and legs of a horse.
charm	Something worn or carried for its magical power. Also, an action said to have magical power.
curse	A spell intended to cause misfortune to another.
djinn	A spirit capable of assuming animal or human form, able to influence humankind for good or evil purposes; genie.

(Continued on next page)

Fantasy / Magic *(continued)*

dragon A winged reptile with crested head and enormous claws and teeth, often spouting fire.

dungeon A strong, dark prison or cell, usually underground.

dwarf A being in the form of a small, often misshapen man, usually having magical powers.

elf A tiny being in human form with magical powers, often mischievous; sprite; fairy.

enchanted Influenced by a charm or spell.

fairy A tiny, graceful being in human form (often with wings) with magical powers.

fairy dust A magical dust used by fairies.

fairy tale A fanciful story, usually involving magical creatures.

faun A creature resembling a man with the ears, horns, tail, and hind legs of a goat.

flying carpet A carpet that will fly people anywhere they wish to go.

(Continued on next page)

Fantasy / Magic *(continued)*

genie A being, often appearing in human form, that grants wishes when summoned by its master; djinn.

giant A being with human form but superhuman size and strength.

gnome A small being, usually described as a shriveled little old man, that inhabits the interior of the earth and acts as a guardian of its treasures.

goblin A grotesque sprite or elf that is mischievous or malicious.

gremlin A mischievous invisible being that causes trouble.

griffin A creature having the head and wings of an eagle and the body of a lion.

grindylow A creature said to inhabit cold water that would grab small children with its long arms and fingers and devour them if they came too close to the edge of a pool, marsh, or pond.

(Continued on next page)

Fantasy / Magic *(continued)*

hag	An ugly old woman, especially a vicious or malicious one; witch or sorceress.
hex	To practice witchcraft on; bewitch.
hippocampus	A monster with the head and front legs of a horse and the tail of a dolphin or other fish.
hobgoblin	A mischievous goblin.
immortality	Unending life.
incantation	The chanting or uttering of words said to have magical power.
legend	A story handed down by tradition and accepted as historical.
leprechaun	A dwarf or sprite said to reveal the location of a hidden pot of gold to whomever catches him.
magic	The art of seeking to manipulate people or events through the use of spells, potions or other techniques.
mermaid	A female marine creature, having the head, torso, and arms of a woman and the tail of a fish.

(Continued on next page)

Fantasy / Magic *(continued)*

muse	A goddess presiding over a particular art such as music, poetry, or dance.
nymph	A beautiful maiden inhabiting the sea, river, woods, trees, mountains, and meadows.
ogre	A hideous giant who feeds on human flesh.
phoenix	A beautiful bird that dies in flames and is reborn from the ashes.
pixie	A fairy or sprite, especially a mischievous one.
potion	A drink said to have magical powers.
runes	Ancient characters inscribed on stones, bones, or other materials; sometimes used to foretell the future.
sasquatch	A very large, hairy, humanlike creature; Big Foot.
sea serpent	An enormous snakelike or dragonlike marine animal.

(Continued on next page)

Fantasy / Magic *(continued)*

seer	A person who can predict future events.
selkie	A creature that looks like a seal in water but assumes human form on land.
shape shifting	The ability of a person or animal to change physical form or shape.
siren	A sea nymph whose singing lures sailors to their death on rocky coasts.
sorcerer	A person who practices sorcery; black magician; wizard.
spell	A word or phrase having magical power.
sphinx	A winged creature with a lion's body and a woman's head. It kills those who cannot answer its riddle.
sprite	An elf, pixie, fairy, or goblin.
talisman	An object believed to bring good luck, or avert evil.
tarot	A set of cards used for fortune telling.

(Continued on next page)

Fantasy / Magic *(continued)*

troll A supernatural being, sometimes a giant and sometimes a dwarf, living in a cave.

unicorn A creature resembling a horse, with a single horn in the center of its forehead.

wand A slender stick or rod with magical powers.

warlock A man who practices magic; a male witch; sorcerer.

witch A woman who practices magic.

wizard A person who practices sorcery, magic.

yeti A hairy, humanlike animal said to inhabit snowy mountains; The Abominable Snowman.

Jungle / Rainforest

adventure	An exciting or very unusual experience.
Amazon	A river in South America, flowing from the Peruvian Andes through Brazil to the Atlantic Ocean.
anaconda	A South American boa that can grow to a length of more than 25 ft (7.9m).
armadillo	Any of several burrowing, mostly nocturnal mammals, having strong claws and a protective covering of bony plates.
baboon	Any of various large, terrestrial monkeys of Africa and Arabia, having a doglike muzzle, large cheek pouches, and a short tail.
binoculars	An optical device used to see in the distance, for use with both eyes, consisting of two small telescopes fitted together side by side.
boa constrictor	A tropical snake that crushes its prey with its coils.

(Continued on next page)

Jungle / Rainforest *(continued)*

botanical	Pertaining to, made from, or containing plants.
branch	A natural subdivision of a plant stem.
bromeliad	Tropical plants having long leaves and showy flowers, including the pineapple and Spanish moss.
brush	A dense growth of bushes or shrubs.
bush	A large area thickly covered with mixed plant growth, trees, etc., as a jungle.
butterfly	Any of a large group of insects characterized by knobbed antennae, a slender body, and large, often brightly colored wings.
camouflage	The act of hiding by some means that alters or obscures the appearance.
camp	A place where a group of persons or an individual is lodged in a tent or tents or other temporary means of shelter.

(Continued on next page)

Jungle / Rainforest *(continued)*

canopy The upper parts of the trees. This leafy environment is full of life in a tropical rainforest and includes: insects, birds, reptiles, mammals, and more.

canteen A small container used for carrying water or other liquids.

chimpanzee An ape of Africa, having a brown-to-black coat, a relatively hairless face with a rounded muzzle, prominent ears, and hands adapted for knuckle-walking, noted for its intelligence and humanlike behavior.

Congo A river in central Africa flowing into the Atlantic.

conservation The act of conserving; prevention of injury, decay, waste, or loss; preservation.

decay To become decomposed; rot.

deforestation To clear of forests or trees.

dense Having parts closely compacted together; crowded.

(Continued on next page)

Jungle / Rainforest *(continued)*

discovery	The act of finding or seeing something new.
diversity	Variety; difference.
drizzle	To rain gently and steadily in fine drops.
emergent	A giant tree that is much higher than the average canopy height. It houses many birds and insects.
endangered	Threatened with extinction.
environment	The air, water, organisms, and all other external factors surrounding and affecting an organism at any time.
equator	The great circle of the earth that is equidistant from the North Pole and South Pole.
expedition	A journey or voyage made for some specific purpose.
fauna	The animals of a given region.

(Continued on next page)

Jungle / Rainforest *(continued)*

fern	Any seedless, non-flowering vascular plant of tropical to temperate regions characterized by true roots, stems, and fronds, and reproducing by spores.
flora	The plants of a particular region.
fly	To move through the air using wings.
forest	A large tract of land covered with trees and underbrush.
forest floor	Ground level, below the understory; teeming with animal life, especially insects. The largest animals in the rainforest generally live here.
fruit	The edible part of a plant developed from a flower.
glide	To move smoothly and continuously along.
gorilla	The largest and most powerful of the apes.
habitat	The natural environment of an organism.

(Continued on next page)

Jungle / Rainforest *(continued)*

hide To conceal from sight; also the pelt or skin of a large animal.

humid Damp or moist.

hunt To chase or search for, usually for the purpose of catching or killing.

hunter One who hunts.

indigenous Originating in and characteristic of a particular region or country; native.

insect Small animal with a body divided into three parts (head, thorax, and abdomen), and having three pairs of legs and usually two pairs of wings; bug.

jaguar A large spotted cat of the tropics, having a tawny coat with black spots.

journey A long trip; traveling from one place to another over great distance.

jump To spring clear of the ground or other support by a sudden muscular effort; leap.

(Continued on next page)

Jungle / Rainforest *(continued)*

jungle Land overgrown with dense trees or vines, especially tropical vegetation or a tropical rainforest.

leaf An outgrowth of a plant stem, usually green.

leap To spring through the air from one point or position to another; jump.

lemur Any of various small, tree-dwelling primates, usually having large eyes, a foxlike face, and woolly fur.

leopard A large, spotted feline, usually tawny with black markings; panther.

limb A large or main branch of a tree.

lizard Any of a group of slender, scaly reptiles with four legs and a tail.

malaria A disease characterized by chills, fever, and sweating; transmitted to humans when bitten by infected mosquitoes.

moist Moderately or slightly wet; damp.

(Continued on next page)

Jungle / Rainforest *(continued)*

mosquito	An insect, the females of which suck the blood of animals and humans, sometimes transmitting disease.
mountain	A natural elevation of the earth's surface having considerable mass, steep sides, and a height greater than a hill.
native	The place or environment in which a person was born or a thing came into being.
nocturnal	Active at night.
nut	A dry fruit consisting of an edible kernel or meat enclosed in a woody or leathery shell.
orangutan	A large, long-armed ape with reddish-brown hair.
parasite	An organism that lives on or within another.
parrot	Any of numerous hook-billed, brilliantly colored birds.
paw	The foot of an animal having claws.

(Continued on next page)

Jungle / Rainforest *(continued)*

piranha	A South American freshwater fish that eats other fish but occasionally also attacks humans and other large animals that enter the water.
poacher	A person who trespasses on private property to catch fish or game illegally.
pounce	To spring suddenly with the intent to catch or grab something.
predator	Any organism that exists by preying upon other organisms.
prey	An organism hunted or seized for food.
provisions	A stock of necessary food or supplies.
python	Any of several boa constrictors often growing to a length of more than 30 feet (9m).
raft	A collection of logs or planks fastened together for floating on water.

(Continued on next page)

Jungle / Rainforest *(continued)*

rain	Water that is condensed from the vapor in the atmosphere and falls to earth in drops.
reptile	Any cold-blooded vertebrate such as turtles, snakes, lizards, crocodiles, etc.
rifle	A shoulder firearm.
river	A natural stream of water of fairly large size flowing in a definite course.
roar	To utter a loud, deep cry or howl.
root	A part of the body of a plant that grows downward into the soil, anchoring the plant and absorbing nutrients and moisture.
sloth	A slow, tree-dwelling mammal that hangs from branches.
snake	A limbless, scaly, elongated reptile that may or may not be venomous.
species	A biological classification composed of related individuals that resemble one another and are able to breed among themselves.

(Continued on next page)

Jungle / Rainforest *(continued)*

spider monkey Any of several tropical monkeys having a slender body, long, slender limbs, and a long tail used for hanging or grasping.

stalk To pursue or approach prey stealthily.

symbiotic The living together of two dissimilar organisms to their mutual advantage.

tail The hindmost part of an animal.

tent A portable shelter of skins, canvas, plastic, or other material supported by one or more poles or a frame and often secured by ropes fastened to pegs in the ground.

territory The area that an animal defends against intruders.

toucan A brightly colored, fruit-eating bird with a very large bill.

tracker One who follows the tracks, traces, or footprints of another.

trek A slow or difficult journey.

(Continued on next page)

Jungle / Rainforest *(continued)*

tribe	A group of people united by ancestors, customs, and traditions.
tropic	Pertaining to, or occurring in the tropics.
understory	A dark, cool environment under the leaves but over the ground.
village	A small community or group of dwellings.
vine	Any plant having a long, weak stem that supports itself by winding around or clinging to other plants or objects.
water	A transparent, odorless, tasteless liquid that constitutes rain, oceans, lakes, rivers, etc.
waterfall	A steep fall or flow of water from a height.
wild	Living in a state of nature; not tamed.
yellow fever	An infectious, often fatal disease caused by a virus transmitted by a mosquito.

Medieval

abbess	A woman who is the superior of a convent of nuns.
abbey	A monastery under the supervision of an abbot or a convent under the supervision of an abbess.
abbot	A man who is the head or superior of a monastery.
ale	A malt beverage, darker, heavier, and more bitter than beer.
alms	Money, food, or other donations given to the poor or needy.
apothecary	A pharmacist.
armor	Any covering worn as a defense against weapons.
arrow	A slender, straight, generally pointed weapon made to be shot from a bow.
barbarian	A person in a savage, primitive state; uncivilized person.
bard	A person who wrote and recited epic or heroic poems, often while playing the harp or lyre.

(Continued on next page)

Medieval *(continued)*

baron A member of the lowest grade of nobility.

barrow A mound of earth or stones placed over a burial site.

bastion A stronghold into which people could go for shelter during a battle.

battering ram A device used for crashing through walls, gates, etc.

bishop A person who oversees a number of churches.

bow A flexible strip of wood bent by a string stretched between its ends, used for shooting arrows.

buttress Any external support built to steady a structure.

Camelot The legendary site of King Arthur's palace and court.

castle A fortified residence, often owned by a prince or noble.

catapult An ancient device used to hurl stones, arrows, etc.

(Continued on next page)

Medieval *(continued)*

cathedral	An important church, sometimes containing a bishop's throne.
chalice	Cup; goblet.
chamber pot	A portable container for urine, used in bedrooms.
chivalry	The ideal characteristics of a knight, including courtesy, generosity, and valor.
clergy	The group of ordained persons in a religion.
constable	An officer of high rank in medieval monarchies, usually the commander of all armed forces, especially in the absence of a ruler.
count	A nobleman equivalent in rank to an English earl.
countess	The wife or widow of a count.
court	The residence of a sovereign or other high dignitary; palace.

(Continued on next page)

Medieval *(continued)*

Crusades	Any of the military expeditions undertaken by European Christians in the 11th, 12th, and 13th centuries to recover the Holy Land from the Muslims.
dagger	A short, swordlike weapon with a pointed blade and a handle.
dragon	A mythical monster generally represented as a huge, winged reptile with crested head and enormous claws and teeth, often spouting fire.
drawbridge	A bridge at the entrance of a castle which can be pulled up or let down.
duchess	The wife or widow of a duke.
duke	A British nobleman holding the highest hereditary title outside the royal family, ranking immediately below a prince.
dungeon	A strong, dark prison or cell, usually underground.

(Continued on next page)

Medieval *(continued)*

earl — A British nobleman of a rank below that of a marquis and above that of a count.

Excalibur — The magic sword of King Arthur.

fair — A regular gathering for barter or sale of goods.

farm — A tract of land on which crops and/or livestock are raised for livelihood.

feud — A bitter, continuous hostility, especially between two families or clans, often lasting for many years or generations.

friar — A male member of a religious order that originally relied solely on alms.

gallows — A wooden frame, consisting of a crossbeam on two uprights, on which condemned persons are executed by hanging.

grail — A cup or chalice that in legend was associated with unusual powers; sought after by medieval knights.

(Continued on next page)

Medieval *(continued)*

great hall The main hall in a castle; used for dining or entertaining.

herald A royal messenger.

heresy Any opinion opposed to established views, especially related to religion.

heretic A person who maintains religious opinions contrary to those accepted by his or her church.

Holy Land The biblical region of Palestine.

infidel A person who does not accept a particular faith, especially Christianity.

jester A professional fool or clown at court.

joust A combat in which two knights on horseback attempt to unhorse each other with blunted lances.

king A male ruler; monarch.

King Arthur A legendary king said to have led the Knights of the Round Table at Camelot.

(Continued on next page)

Medieval *(continued)*

kingdom	A state or government having a king or queen as its ruler.
Knights of the Round Table	A legendary order of knights created by King Arthur.
lady	A woman of high social position.
lady-in-waiting	A lady who is in attendance upon a queen or princess.
lance	A long wooden shaft with a pointed metal head, used as a weapon by knights.
lord	A person who has authority or control over others.
lyre	A stringed instrument of the harp family having two curved arms connected at the upper end by a crossbar, used to accompany a singer or bard.
maid	A young girl or unmarried woman. Also, a girl or woman servant.
maiden	A young girl or unmarried woman.
manor	An estate upon acres of land.

(Continued on next page)

Medieval *(continued)*

march	To walk with regular and measured steps, as soldiers on parade.
marquis	A nobleman ranking next below a duke and above an earl or count.
marquise	A wife or widow of a marquis.
mead	An alcoholic liquor made by fermenting honey and water.
merchant	A person who buys and sells commodities for profit.
Merlin	A wise magician and seer.
minstrel	A poet and musician who sings or recites while accompanying himself on a stringed instrument.
moat	A deep, wide trench, usually filled with water, surrounding the rampart of a fortified place such as a castle.
monarch	A ruler of a state or nation.
monastery	A place of residence occupied by a group of religious persons, especially monks.

(Continued on next page)

Medieval *(continued)*

monk	A man who has withdrawn from the world for religious reasons.
mortar	A receptacle of hard material, having a bowl-shaped cavity in which substances are reduced to powder with a pestle.
nobleman	A man of noble birth or rank.
nunnery	A building or group of buildings for nuns; convent.
oxen	Plural of ox. Cud-chewing mammals of the cattle family used to pull heavy loads.
page	A youth being trained for knighthood. A boy servant or attendant.
parapet	A defensive wall or elevation, as of earth or stone used as a shield from enemy fire.
peasant	A farmer or laborer of low social rank.
pence	Plural of penny (pennies).
penny	Bronze coin; the 12th part of a shilling.

(Continued on next page)

Medieval *(continued)*

pestle	A tool for pounding or grinding substances in a mortar.
plague	A disease that causes widespread death.
pound	Also called pound sterling. A nickel-brass coin, formerly equal to 20 shillings or 240 pence.
prince	A son of a king or queen.
princess	A daughter of a king or queen.
pub	A bar or tavern.
queen	A female ruler; monarch.
quest	A search or pursuit made in order to find or obtain something.
rack	Instrument of torture consisting of a framework on which a victim was tied by the wrists and ankles to be slowly stretched.
rampart	An elevation or mound of earth raised as a fortification around a place.
rat	Long-tailed rodent.
realm	A royal domain.

(Continued on next page)

Medieval *(continued)*

renaissance The time of the great revival of art, literature, and learning in Europe beginning in the 14th century and extending to the 17th century, marking the transition from the medieval to the modern world.

seer A person who predicts future events.

serf A servant; a person bound to a master's land.

sheriff An important civil officer in a shire.

shield A broad piece of armor, carried apart from the body as a defense against swords, lances, and arrows.

shilling A coin equal to the 20th part of a pound, equal to 12 pence.

shire One of the counties of Great Britain.

(Continued on next page)

Medieval *(continued)*

siege The act of surrounding and attacking a fortified place in such a way as to isolate it from help and supplies for the purpose of making capture possible.

sorcerer A person who practices sorcery or magic; a wizard.

sovereign A monarch; a king, queen, or other ruler.

squire A young nobleman who serves a knight, hoping to become one someday.

sword A weapon having various forms but consisting typically of a long, straight, or slightly curved blade with one end pointed and the other fixed in a handle.

tavern A public house for travelers and others; inn.

templar A member of a religious military order founded by Crusaders around 1118 A.D. and suppressed in 1312 A.D.

(Continued on next page)

Medieval *(continued)*

throne	The chair or seat occupied by a sovereign, bishop, or other exalted person.
tower	A high structure, usually part of another building.
trebuchet	A device of war with a sling used for hurling missiles such as large boulders.
turret	A small tower, usually one forming part of a larger structure.
wench	A country lass or female servant.
wizard	A person who practices magic; magician or sorcerer.
yoke	A device for joining together a pair of draft animals, especially oxen.

Mythology

Acropolis	The citadel or high fortified area of ancient Athens.
Aeneas	A Trojan hero, the reputed ancestor of the Romans; protagonist of the Aeneid.
Agamemnon	A king of Mycenae, a son of Atreus and brother of Menelaus. He led the Greeks in the Trojan War and was murdered by Clytemnestra, his wife, upon his return from Troy.
ally	A friendly nation; someone who provides cooperation or assistance.
Amazon	A member of a race of female warriors said to live near the Black Sea.
ambrosia	The food of the gods.
amphitheater	An oval or round building with tiers of seats around a central open area; arena; stadium.
Aphrodite	The Greek goddess of love and beauty. Roman name: Venus.

(Continued on next page)

Mythology *(continued)*

Apollo The Greek and Roman god of light, healing, music, poetry, prophecy, and manly beauty.

archer A person who shoots with a bow and arrow; bowman.

Ares The Greek god of war, a son of Zeus and Hera. Roman name: Mars.

Argonaut One who sailed with Jason on his ship, Argo, in search of the Golden Fleece.

armor Any covering worn as a defense against weapons.

Artemis A Greek goddess, the daughter of Leto and the sister of Apollo, characterized as a huntress and associated with the moon.

Atalanta A huntress who promised to marry the man who could win a foot race against her.

Athena The Greek goddess of wisdom and fertility. At birth she sprang forth fully armed from the head of her father, Zeus.

(Continued on next page)

Mythology *(continued)*

Atlas A Titan, condemned to support the heavens on his shoulders.

boat A vessel for transport by water.

bow A flexible strip of wood bent by a string stretched between its ends, used for shooting arrows.

chariot A light, two-wheeled vehicle for one person, usually drawn by two horses and driven from a standing position, used in warfare, racing, hunting etc.

chimaeras Also chimera. A fire-breathing monster usually represented as a composite of a lion, goat, and serpent.

chiton A gown or tunic, with or without sleeves, worn by men and women in ancient Greece.

clouds A visible body of very fine water droplets or ice particles suspended in the atmosphere.

Coliseum The amphitheater of Rome, the largest in the world.

(Continued on next page)

Mythology *(continued)*

Cronus A Titan and the father of Zeus. Roman name: Saturn.

cyclops A member of a family of giants having a single round eye in the middle of the forehead.

Daphne A nymph who, when pursued by Apollo, was saved by being changed into a laurel tree.

deity A god or goddess.

Demeter The Greek goddess of harvest and the protector of marriage. Roman name: Ceres.

Dionysus The Greek god of fertility and wine. Roman name: Bacchus.

dryad A deity presiding over woods and trees; a wood nymph.

Echo A mountain nymph who loved her own voice. It is said that she angered the goddess Hera, who punished Echo by taking away her voice, except in repetition of another's shouted words.

(Continued on next page)

Mythology *(continued)*

enemy	A person who feels hatred for or wishes to harm another; an adversary or opponent.
Eros	The Greek god of love, represented as a winged youth armed with a bow and arrows. The son of Aphrodite. Roman name: Cupid.
fate	Something that unavoidably befalls a person; fortune.
Furies	Three snake-haired monsters who pursued unpunished criminals.
Gaea	Also, Gaia. The Greek goddess of the earth and mother of the Titans; Mother Earth.
Galatea	A maiden who had been an ivory statue carved by Pygmalion and brought to life by Aphrodite in response to his prayers.
god	A supreme being; male deity.
goddess	A female god.
gold	A precious yellow metallic element.

(Continued on next page)

Mythology *(continued)*

Golden Age	The first and best of the four ages of humankind; an era of peace and innocence.
Golden Fleece	The pure gold fleece pursued by Jason and the Argonauts.
gorgon	Any of three sister monsters commonly represented as having snakes for hair and eyes that would turn anyone looking into them to stone.
Graiae	Three witch sisters with one eye and one tooth shared among them.
Hades	The underworld inhabited by departed souls. Ruled by Pluto.
healer	A person or thing that heals.
Helios	The Greek god of the sun, represented as driving a chariot across the heavens. Roman name: Sol.
helmet	Protective head covering worn by soldiers.
Hephaestus	The Greek god of fire, metalworking, and handicrafts. Roman name: Vulcan.

(Continued on next page)

Mythology *(continued)*

Hera Greek queen of heaven and wife of Zeus.

Heracles A celebrated hero possessing exceptional strength. Said to be the son of Zeus. Also known as Hercules.

Hermes The Greek herald and messenger of the gods; the god of roads, commerce, and invention. Roman name: Mercury.

hero A man of distinguished courage or ability, admired for his brave deeds and noble qualities.

heroine A woman of distinguished courage or ability, admired for her brave deeds and noble qualities.

Hestia The Greek goddess of the hearth.

immortal Living forever. Also, a being who lives forever.

Jason A hero and leader of the Argonauts who retrieved the Golden Fleece and slew Medusa.

(Continued on next page)

Mythology *(continued)*

labyrinth	An intricate combination of paths or passages in which it is difficult to find one's way or to reach the exit; maze.
laurel	A small European evergreen tree having dark, glossy green leaves. Often used to create a wreath placed on the head to symbolize victory or distinction.
Leto	Loved by Zeus; the mother of Apollo and Artemis. Roman name: Latona.
Lyre	A small string instrument of ancient Greece similar to a harp; used to accompany singing or reciting.
maiden	A girl or young unmarried woman.
Medusa	The only mortal Gorgon. She was once a beautiful woman, but she offended Athena, who changed her hair into snakes and made her face so hideous that all who looked at her were turned to stone.

(Continued on next page)

Mythology *(continued)*

Midas — A king who was given the power of turning whatever he touched into gold.

minotaur — A creature with the head of a bull on the body of a man.

moon — The earth's natural satellite.

Mount Olympus — A mountain in Greece; mythical home of the Greek gods.

Naiads — Nymphs presiding over rivers and springs.

Narcissus — A young man who pined away in love for his own image in a pool of water and was transformed into a flower.

nectar — The life-giving drink of the gods.

Nemesis — The goddess of divine retribution; the avenger of the gods. Also: nemesis, an opponent or rival one cannot best or overcome.

Nereid — A sea nymph.

Nereus — A sea god and father of the Nereids.

(Continued on next page)

Mythology *(continued)*

Ocean	A Titan, son of Heaven (Uranus) and Gaia (Earth). He was father to the Oceanids and the river gods.
Odysseus	One of the heroes of the Iliad and protagonist of the Odyssey; shrewdest of the Greek leaders in the Trojan War.
Oedipus	A king of Thebes: as was prophesied at his birth, he unwittingly killed his father and married his mother and, in penance, blinded himself.
Olympians	Relating to the greater gods and goddesses of ancient Greece who lived on Mount Olympus.
oracle	A person who delivers responses of a god or goddess to a request or question.

(Continued on next page)

Mythology *(continued)*

Orpheus — A poet and musician, who followed his dead wife, Eurydice, to the underworld. By charming Hades, he obtained permission to lead her away, provided he did not look back at her until they returned to earth. But at the last moment he looked, and she was lost to him forever.

Ouranos — The personification of Heaven and ruler of the world; father of the Titans. Roman name: Uranus.

Pan — A god of forests, pastures, flocks, and shepherds, represented with the head, chest, and arms of a man and the legs, horns, and ears of a goat.

Pandora — The first woman, created by Hephaestus, presented to Epimetheus along with a box which contained all the evils that could trouble humanity. As the gods had anticipated, Pandora gave in to her curiosity and opened the box, allowing the evils to escape.

(Continued on next page)

Mythology *(continued)*

Pantheon	A domed circular temple in Rome.
Parthenon	The temple of Athena on the Acropolis in Athens.
peace	The condition of a nation or people not at war.
Pegasus	A winged horse, created from the blood of Medusa.
Perseus	A hero, the son of Zeus and Danae, who slew the Gorgon Medusa, and afterward saved Andromeda from a sea monster.
Phaeton	The son of Helios. He tried to drive his father's sun-chariot but crashed after nearly setting fire to the earth.
plague	A disease that causes widespread death.
Poseidon	The Greek god of the sea, with the power to cause earthquakes. He was the brother of Zeus. Roman name: Neptune.
priest	A man having the authority or power to administer religious rites.

(Continued on next page)

Mythology *(continued)*

priestess	A woman having the authority or power to administer religious rites.
Prometheus	A Titan who taught humankind various arts and was said to have shaped humans out of clay and given them the spark of life. He also gave humankind fire stolen from Olympus in defiance of Zeus for which he was severely punished.
prophecy	The foretelling or prediction of future events.
protector	A person or thing that protects; defender; guardian.
Proteus	A sea god, noted for his ability to assume different forms and to tell the future.

(Continued on next page)

Mythology *(continued)*

Psyche The beautiful young woman loved by Eros. He swept her off to a lovely castle but forbade her to look at him since he was a god. When she disobeyed, he left her, but she ceaselessly searched for him, performing difficult and dangerous tasks, until at last she was reunited with him forever and made immortal.

Pygmalion King of Cyprus. He fell in love with a beautiful statue of a woman. When he prayed to Aphrodite for a wife like it, the goddess brought the statue to life and Pygmalion married her.

revenge To inflict harm in return of a mental or physical injury.

River Styx A river in Hades across which dead souls were ferried.

ruins The remains of a building or city that has been destroyed or that is in a state of decay.

sacred Devoted or dedicated to a deity or to some religious purpose.

(Continued on next page)

Mythology *(continued)*

sacrifice The offering of animal, plant, or human life or of some material possession to a deity.

satyr A woodland deity, represented as part human, part horse, and sometimes part goat.

scroll A roll of parchment, paper, copper, or other material, especially one with writing on it.

sea The salt waters that cover the greater part of the earth's surface.

shield A broad piece of armor, carried apart from the body, usually on the left arm, as a defense against swords, lances, arrows, etc.

sorrow Distress caused by loss or disappointment; grief, sadness.

spring A flow of water rising from the ground, forming a small stream or pool of water.

(Continued on next page)

Mythology *(continued)*

sword	A weapon having various forms but consisting typically of a long, straight or slightly curved blade with one end pointed and the other fixed in a handle.
temple	A place dedicated to the service or worship of a deity or deities.
thunder	A loud, explosive noise produced by the expansion of air heated by a lightning discharge.
thunderbolt	A flash of lightning with the accompanying thunder; a bolt cast to earth in a flash of lightning.
Titans	The primeval deities defeated by Zeus and his brothers.
transform	To change form or appearance.
trident	Three-pronged fork carried by Poseidon.
Triton	Son of Poseidon, represented as having the head and trunk of a man and tail of a fish.
Trojan	A citizen of the city of Troy.

(Continued on next page)

Mythology *(continued)*

Troy An ancient city made famous by Homer's account of the Trojan War.

tunic A gownlike garment, with or without sleeves and sometimes belted, worn by the ancient Greeks and Romans.

vengeance Infliction of injury, harm, or humiliation on a person by another who has been harmed by that person; violent revenge.

war A conflict carried on by force of arms, as between nations.

warrior A person engaged or experienced in warfare; soldier.

woods A dense growth of trees or underbrush covering a relatively small or confined area; a forest.

Zeus The supreme deity of the ancient Greeks. Roman name: Jupiter.

Ocean / Island

adrift	Floating without control; not anchored.
anchor	A device dropped by a chain or rope to the bottom of a body of water to prevent or restrict the motion of a vessel or other floating object.
anemone	A marine animal having a columnar body and one or more circles of tentacles surrounding the mouth.
bay	A body of water forming an indentation of the shoreline, larger than a cove.
beach	An expanse of sand or pebble along a shore.
boat	A vessel for transport by water.
breakwater	A barrier that breaks the force of waves.
breeze	A light wind or current of air.
calm	Freedom from motion or disturbance; stillness.

(Continued on next page)

Ocean / Island *(continued)*

captain A person who is in authority over others; master of a ship; chief; leader.

cave A hollow in the earth with one or more openings horizontal into a hill, mountain, etc.

clam A hard-shelled mollusk, often used for food.

cliff A high, steep face of a rock.

clouds A visible body of very fine water droplets or ice particles suspended in the atmosphere.

coconut The large, hard-shelled seed of the coconut palm, lined with a white edible meat, and containing a milky liquid.

compass An instrument for determining directions which uses a rotating magnetized needle to indicate magnetic north.

coral The hard, colorful skeleton secreted by some marine creatures.

cove A small indentation or recess in the shoreline of a sea, lake, or river.

(Continued on next page)

Ocean / Island *(continued)*

crab A crustacean having eyes on short stalks, a broad, flattened body, four sets of legs, and two pincers.

crustacean A marine creature typically having a body covered with a hard shell or crust, including lobsters, shrimps, crabs, barnacles, etc.

current A large portion of air, large body of water, etc., moving in a certain direction.

cuttlefish A sea creature having eight arms with suckers and two tentacles, and ejecting a black, inky fluid when in danger.

dinghy Any of various small boats, usually found on larger vessels.

dolphin A marine mammal having a fishlike body, numerous teeth, and a head elongated into a beaklike snout.

eel Any of numerous elongated, snakelike marine or freshwater fishes.

(Continued on next page)

Ocean / Island *(continued)*

erupt	To burst forth; to eject matter (of a volcano, geyser, etc.)
fathom	A unit of length equal to six feet (1.8 meters): used chiefly in nautical measurements.
fin	A winglike or paddle-like organ attached to a part of the body of fishes and certain other aquatic animals, used for propulsion, steering, or balancing.
fire	A burning mass of material.
fish	Any of various cold-blooded, aquatic animals, having gills, commonly fins, and typically an elongated body covered with scales.
float	To rest or remain on the surface of a liquid. Also, something that floats, as a raft.
gale	A very strong wind.
gust	A sudden, strong blast of wind.
hammock	A hanging bed or couch made of canvas or netted cord and attached to supports at each end.

(Continued on next page)

Ocean / Island *(continued)*

harbor A part of a body of water along the shore deep enough for anchoring a ship and situated to provide protection from winds, waves, and currents.

harpoon A barbed, spearlike missile attached to a rope, and thrown by hand or shot from a gun, used for killing and capturing whales and large fish. Also to strike, catch, or kill with a harpoon.

horizon The line that appears to be the boundary between earth and sky.

hurricane A violent, tropical storm having wind speeds of or in excess of 72mph (32m/sec).

hut A small dwelling of simple construction, especially one made of natural materials.

island A tract of land completely surrounded by water, and not large enough to be called a continent.

(Continued on next page)

Ocean / Island *(continued)*

jellyfish — A marine creature with a soft, gelatinous structure, usually with an umbrella-like body and long, trailing tentacles.

jungle — A wild land overgrown with dense vegetation, often nearly impenetrable, especially tropical vegetation or a tropical rain forest.

kelp — Any large, cold-water seaweed.

lagoon — An area of shallow water separated from the sea by low sandy dunes.

lean-to — A shack or shed supported at one side by trees or posts and having an inclined roof.

lobster — A large, edible marine crustacean having four sets of legs and a set of large pincers.

maroon — To put ashore on a deserted island with little hope of rescue or escape.

mermaid — A female marine creature found in folklore, said to have the head, torso, and arms of a woman and the tail of a fish.

(Continued on next page)

Ocean / Island *(continued)*

monsoon	The seasonal wind of the Indian Ocean and southern Asia. Also, the rainy season during which this wind blows from the southwest.
moonlight	The light of the moon.
native	Being the place in which a person or creature was born or a plant grown; an original inhabitant.
octopus	A sea creature having a soft, oval body and eight arms covered with suckers.
palm	A plant having a branchless trunk crowned by large leaves at the top.
pelican	A large, fish-eating bird, having a large bill with a pouch.
penguin	Any of several flightless, aquatic birds of the Southern Hemisphere, having webbed feet and wings used as flippers.
pirate	A person who robs or commits violence at sea or on the shores of the sea.

(Continued on next page)

Ocean / Island *(continued)*

puffer fish	A marine fish whose elongated, spiny body can inflate itself with water or air to form a globe; several species contain a potent nerve poison.
raft	A rigid floating platform made of materials such as logs or planks bound together.
rain	Water that is condensed from the vapor in the atmosphere and falls to earth in drops.
ray	A fish with a flat, broad body, wide fins on each side, and a whiplike tail.
reef	A ridge of rocks, sand, or coral, on or near the surface of the water.
rescue	To free from confinement, violence, danger, or evil. Also, the act of rescuing.
roar	To utter a loud, deep cry or howl.
sail	An area of canvas or other fabric spread to catch the wind to drive along a boat or ship. Also, to move along or travel over water.

(Continued on next page)

Ocean / Island *(continued)*

sailor	One who sails.
salt	A mineral found in seawater.
sand	The tiny grains of pulverized rock found on beaches.
scuba	A portable breathing device for underwater divers. (Self-Contained Underwater Breathing Apparatus)
sea	The salt waters that cover the greater part of the earth's surface; ocean.
sea horse	A small, plated fish with an elongated body, a curled tail, and a head resembling a horse.
sea lion	Any of several large eared seals of the northern Pacific.
sea shell	The shell of any marine creature.
sea snake	A venomous marine snake.
sea star	A marine creature having a body usually in the form of a star, with five or more rays or arms radiating from a central disk. Also known as a starfish.

(Continued on next page)

Ocean / Island *(continued)*

sea turtle Any of several large turtles, widely distributed in tropical and subtropical seas, having paddle-like flippers.

sea urchin A sea creature having a somewhat spherical shape and a shell composed of many plates covered with projecting spines.

seagull A water bird, usually gray and white, with webbed feet found mostly near the coast.

seal A marine mammal with a torpedo-shaped body and four flippers.

seaweed Any plant or plants growing in the ocean.

shade The darkness caused by the screening of rays of light.

shark A large, predatory sea fish.

shelter Something beneath, behind, or within which a person, animal, or thing is protected from storms or other adverse conditions.

(Continued on next page)

Ocean / Island *(continued)*

ship A vessel, especially a large oceangoing one propelled by sails or engines.

shipwreck The destruction or loss of a ship, as by sinking; the remains of a wrecked ship.

shore The land along the edge of a sea, lake, broad river, etc.

shoreline The line where shore and water meet.

snorkel A hard rubber or plastic tube through which a swimmer can breathe while moving at or just below the surface of the water. Also, to engage in snorkeling.

spyglass A small telescope.

squall A sudden, violent gust of wind, often accompanied by rain, snow, or sleet.

squid A sea creature having a slender body and ten arms, two longer than the others.

(Continued on next page)

Ocean / Island *(continued)*

stingray	Any of the rays, having a long, flexible tail armed with a strong, bony spine with which they can inflict painful wounds.
storm	A disturbance of the normal condition of the atmosphere causing winds of unusual force, often accompanied by rain, snow, hail, thunder, and lightning, or flying sand or dust.
stranded	Cut off or left behind.
sun	The star that is the central body of the solar system, around which the planets revolve and from which they receive light and heat.
sunstroke	A condition caused by too much exposure to the sun, causing fever and collapse.
surf	The swell of the sea that breaks upon a shore. Also, to ride a surfboard.
tentacle	A slender, flexible appendage used by an animal as an organ of touch; feeler.

(Continued on next page)

Ocean / Island *(continued)*

thirst	A sensation of dryness in the mouth and throat caused by the need for liquid.
tidal wave	A large, destructive ocean wave, produced by a seaquake, hurricane, or strong wind.
tide	The periodic rise and fall of the waters of the ocean and its inlets, produced by the attraction of the moon and sun, and occurring about every 12 hours.
treasure chest	A chest filled with valuables.
tropical	Pertaining to or characteristic of the tropics.
tsunami	An unusually large sea wave produced by a seaquake or undersea volcanic eruption.
uninhabited	Having no residents.
volcano	A vent in the earth's crust through which lava, steam, ash, and debris are expelled.
water	A transparent, odorless, tasteless liquid that constitutes rain, oceans, lakes, rivers, etc.

(Continued on next page)

Ocean / Island *(continued)*

waterfall	A steep fall or flow of water from a height.
wave	A disturbance on the surface of a liquid body, as the sea.
whale	A large marine mammal having a fishlike body, flippers, and a head that is flattened.
white caps	A wave with a crest of foam.

Pirates

addled	Mad, insane; confused.
aft	Toward the rear of the ship.
ahoy	Hello.
avast	Who goes there?
belay	Stop, as in "Belay that order," meaning disregard that order.
bilge rat	The bilge is the lowest part of the ship inside the hull where stinking bilge water collects. A bilge rat is a rat that lives in the bilge. Used as an insult.
black spot	To sentence a pirate to death or to warn him he is marked for death.
blimey	An exclamation of surprise.
booty	Loot; treasure.
bosun	A petty officer.
bowsprit	The slanted pole at a ship's prow.
briny deep	The ocean.
buccaneer	A term for Caribbean pirates.
bucko	Friend.
cap'n	Short for captain.

(Continued on next page)

Pirates *(continued)*

chest	Treasure container.
crow's nest	An enclosed platform near the top of a mast where a lookout would watch for ships or land.
cutlass	A curved sword, like a saber only heavier.
Davy Jones' Locker	The bottom of the sea.
dog	A mild insult, perhaps a friendly one.
doubloon	A Spanish gold coin.
flogging	Punishment by caning or by whipping.
fore	Toward the front of the boat.
gangway	"Get out of my way."
Godspeed	"Goodbye, good luck."
grog	Any alcoholic drink.
grub	Food.
hands	Crew of a ship; sailors.
head	Toilet aboard a ship.

(Continued on next page)

Pirates *(continued)*

Jolly Roger	The pirates' skull-and-crossbones flag.
keelhaul	Punishment by dragging under the ship from one side to the other.
lad	A young boy.
landlubber	A bad or inexperienced sailor.
lass or **lassie**	A young girl.
lookout	Someone posted to keep watch for other ships or land.
maroon	To put ashore on a deserted island with little hope of rescue or escape.
matey	A cheerful way to address someone.
me hearties	A way for a pirate to address his crew.
ocean	The vast body of salt water that covers almost three fourths of the earth's surface.
piece of eight	A Spanish silver coin.
pirate	A seagoing robber or murderer.
plank	A long, think board laid over the ship's side, used to execute enemies.

(Continued on next page)

Pirates *(continued)*

poop deck	The highest deck at the aft of a large ship.
port	A place in a harbor where ships load and unload cargo. Also, the left side of the ship.
prow	The nose of the ship.
reef	An underwater obstruction of rock or coral.
rum	Traditional pirate drink.
saber	A heavy, one-edged sword that is slightly curved.
salt or **old salt**	An experienced seaman.
savvy	Do you understand?
scuppers	Openings along the edges of a ship's deck that allow water to drain back to the sea.
scurvy	A disease that afflicted sailors, caused by lack of vitamin C.
sea	The salt waters that cover the greater part of the earth's surface.
sea dog	An experienced seaman.
shanty	A sea song.

(Continued on next page)

Pirates *(continued)*

shipshape Well organized, under control.

spyglass A telescope.

swab To clean something, such as the decks of a ship.

wench A derogatory term for a young woman; a female servant.

yo-ho-ho Used as a call or shout or to call attention.

Prehistoric

Allosaurus Meaning "strange lizard." A carnivorous dinosaur of the late Jurassic and early Cretaceous Periods, similar to but smaller than the Tyrannosaur.

ancestor The form or stock from which an organism has developed or descended.

Ankylosaurus Meaning "crooked lizard." A large herbivorous dinosaur of the Cretaceous Period, having a squat, heavily armored body and a clubbed tail.

Apatosaurus Meaning "deceptive lizard." A very large herbivorous dinosaur of the late Jurassic Period, having a long neck and tail and a relatively small head.

Archaeopteryx Meaning "primitive wing." A reptile-like bird from the late Jurassic Period, having teeth and a long, feathered, vertebrate tail.

armor Any protective covering.

artifact Any object made by human beings.

(Continued on next page)

Prehistoric *(continued)*

biped A two-footed animal.

Brachiosaurus Meaning "arm lizard." A massive herbivorous sauropod dinosaur of the Jurassic and Cretaceous Periods, having a long flexible neck, nostrils above the eyes, and forelegs that were much longer than the hind legs.

brooding To sit on or hatch eggs; to protect young by covering with the wings.

carnivore An animal that eats flesh.

Carnotaurus Meaning "meat-bull." A large predatory dinosaur with horns vaguely resembling a bull's.

catastrophic event An event causing mass extinction; thought to be the cause of the fall of the dinosaurs.

cave A hollow in the earth, especially one opening more or less horizontally into a hill, mountain, etc.

(Continued on next page)

Prehistoric *(continued)*

Ceratosaurus	Meaning "horned lizard." Medium sized theropod of the Jurassic period; swift-running carnivorous dinosaur having grasping hands with sharp claws and a short horn between the nostrils.
claw	A sharp, curved nail at the end of a toe of a mammal, reptile, or bird.
Coelophysis	Meaning "hollow form." One of the oldest known dinosaurs of the late Triassic Period; a small, hollow-boned, carnivorous biped from North America.
continent	One of the main landmasses of the globe (Europe, Asia, Africa, North America, South America, Australia, and Antarctica).
crest	A ridge or ridgelike formation, especially on a bone.

(Continued on next page)

Prehistoric *(continued)*

Cretaceous Pertaining to a period of the Mesozoic Era, from 140 million to 65 million years ago, characterized by the greatest development and subsequent extinction of dinosaurs and the appearance of flowering plants and modern insects.

Deinonychus Meaning "terrible claw." A small bipedal dinosaur of the Cretaceous Period, having a large, curved claw on each hind foot.

descendent Deriving or descending from an ancestor.

desert A region so arid because of little rainfall that it supports only sparse vegetation or no vegetation at all.

devour To swallow or eat up hungrily, voraciously, or ravenously.

(Continued on next page)

Prehistoric *(continued)*

Dilophosaurus Meaning "two-crested reptile." The largest carnivorous dinosaur found in North America, with two crests that extend upward from the nostrils and run back along the top of the head. Its long, powerful hind limbs indicate the ability to run fast and the toes, tipped by long claws, allowed it to grip the ground and to pin down its prey.

dinosaur Any herbivorous or carnivorous reptile from the Mesozoic Era.

Diplodocus Meaning "double beam." An immense herbivorous dinosaur from the Late Jurassic Period, growing to a length of about 87 ft. (26.5 m). It had a long whiplike tail and small horselike head with nostrils placed just below and between the eyes.

discovery To be the first to find or learn something.

(Continued on next page)

Prehistoric *(continued)*

dive	To plunge into water, especially headfirst; to plunge or fall through the air.
egg	The roundish reproductive body produced by the female of animals such as birds and some reptiles.
epoch	A particular period of time marked by distinctive features, events, etc.
era	A major division of geologic time composed of a number of periods.
evolution	Change in the gene pool of a population from generation to generation by such processes as mutation and natural selection.
excavate	To dig or scoop out (earth, sand, etc.).
extinct	No longer in existence; died out.
feather	A soft, light growth covering the body of a bird, often assists in flying.
fern	A seedless, non-flowering plant having roots, stems, and fronds, and reproducing by spores.

(Continued on next page)

Prehistoric *(continued)*

flood	A great flowing or overflowing of water, especially over land not usually under water.
fly	To move through the air using wings. Also, any of numerous two-winged insects such as the common housefly.
fossil	The preserved remains, impression, or trace of a living thing, as a skeleton, footprint, etc.
frill	A bony plate that curves upward behind the skull of many dinosaurs.
hatch	To bring forth from the egg.
herbivore	An animal that feeds chiefly on plants.
horn	One of the bony, permanent growths, often curved and pointed, that project from the upper part of the head of certain animals.
hunt	To chase or search, usually for the purpose of catching or killing.
hunter	One who hunts.

(Continued on next page)

Prehistoric *(continued)*

Iguanodon Meaning "iguana tooth." A plant-eating dinosaur that lived in the Cretaceous Period characterized by teeth similar to those of the iguana, a horny beak, spikelike thumbs, and a powerful tail. It grew to a length of 15 to 30 ft (4.5 to 9 m) and may have been capable of walking on either two or four feet.

invertebrate Any animal lacking a backbone.

jaw Either of two bones forming the framework of the mouth.

Jurassic Pertaining to a period of the Mesozoic Era, occurring from 190 to 140 million years ago and characterized by an abundance of dinosaurs and the appearance of birds and mammals.

lagoon An area of shallow water separated from the sea by low sand dunes.

Maiasaura Meaning "good mother lizard." A large duck-billed dinosaur that lived in the Cretaceous Period.

(Continued on next page)

Prehistoric *(continued)*

Mastodon Meaning "nipple tooth." A massive, elephant-like mammal having long, curved upper tusks and, in the male, short lower tusks.

Megalosaurus Meaning "great lizard." A large carnivorous theropod dinosaur of the Jurassic Period.

Mesozoic Pertaining to an era occurring between 230 and 650 million years ago, characterized by the appearance of flowering plants and by the appearance and extinction of dinosaurs.

meteor A meteoroid which is entering Earth's atmosphere from space; called a meteorite after landing.

migrate To go from one country, region, or place to another.

Mosasaur A carnivorous marine lizard from the Cretaceous Period, having limbs resembling broad, webbed paddles.

(Continued on next page)

Prehistoric *(continued)*

nest	A pocketlike structure of twigs, grass, mud, etc, formed as a place in which to lay and hatch eggs and rear young.
ocean	The vast body of salt water that covers almost three fourths of the earth's surface.
omnivore	An animal that feeds on both animals and plants.
Oviraptor	Meaning "egg thief." A small theropod of the Cretaceous Period with a short domed skull, a toothless beak, and a unique head crest.
Pachycephalo-saurus	Meaning "thick-headed lizard." A bipedal herbivore having 10 inches (25.4 cm) of bone atop its head; largest boneheaded dinosaur ever found.
pack	A group of certain animals of the same kind, especially predatory ones.
paleontologist	A scientist who studies fossils to understand the forms of life existing in former geologic periods.

(Continued on next page)

Prehistoric *(continued)*

Pangaea	The hypothetical landmass that existed when all continents were joined.
Parasaurolophus	Meaning "beside the lizard crest." One of the rarest of the duck-billed dinosaurs; an herbivorous dinosaur from the Cretaceous Period that could walk on either two or four feet.
period	A rather large interval of time that is meaningful in the life of a person, in history, etc., because of its particular characteristics.
petroglyph	A drawing or carving on rock, made by a member of a prehistoric people.
pictograph	A record consisting of pictorial symbols, such as a prehistoric cave drawing.
Plesiosaur	Meaning "near lizard." A marine reptile from the Jurassic and Cretaceous Periods, having a small head, a long neck, four paddle-like limbs, and a short tail.

(Continued on next page)

Prehistoric *(continued)*

predator Any organism that exists by preying upon other organisms.

prehistoric Pertaining to the time prior to recorded history.

preserve To keep in perfect or unaltered condition; maintain unchanged.

prey An organism hunted or seized for food.

quadruped An animal having four feet.

sauropod Herbivorous dinosaurs from the Jurassic and Cretaceous Periods, having a small head, long neck and tail, and five-toed limbs: the largest known land animal.

scavenger An animal or other organism that feeds on dead organic matter.

shred To cut or tear into small pieces.

shrub A woody plant smaller than a tree, usually having multiple stems branching from or near the ground.

skin The external covering of an animal body.

(Continued on next page)

Prehistoric *(continued)*

skull The bony framework of the head, enclosing the brain and supporting the face.

snake A limbless, scaly, elongated reptile that may or may not be venomous.

species A class of individuals having some common characteristics or qualities.

spike A sharp, pointed projection.

spine A stiff, pointed projection on an animal.

stalk To pursue or approach prey stealthily.

Stegosaurus Meaning "roofed reptile." An herbivorous dinosaur of the Jurassic to the Cretaceous Periods, having a double row of upright bony plates along the back, long hind legs, a short neck, and a small head.

(Continued on next page)

Prehistoric *(continued)*

Styracosaurus Meaning "spike lizard'. A dinosaur of the Cretaceous Period having many large spikes around the edge of its bony frill and a long nose horn.

swim To move in water by movements of the limbs, fins, tail, etc.

talon A claw of a predatory animal.

tar pit An accumulation of natural tar that acts as a trap into which animals have fallen and sunk, preserving their bones.

tear To pull apart or in pieces by force.

thunder To make a loud, resounding noise like the thunder that comes with a storm.

theropod Carnivorous dinosaurs that had short forelimbs and walked or ran on their hind legs.

tooth One of the hard structures usually attached in a row to each jaw, used to tear and chew food and as weapons of attack or defense.

(Continued on next page)

Prehistoric *(continued)*

Triassic Pertaining to a period of the Mesozoic Era, occurring from 230 to 190 million years ago and characterized by the appearance of dinosaurs and coniferous forests.

Triceratops Meaning "three-horned face." The largest of the horned dinosaurs of the Cretaceous Period, having a bony crest on the neck, a long horn over each eye, and a shorter horn on the nose.

Tyrannosaurus Meaning "tyrant lizard." A very large bipedal carnivore of the Cretaceous Period, characterized by small forelimbs, strong hind limbs, a muscular tail, and a large head.

Velociraptor Meaning "swift robber." A fast bipedal carnivore of the Cretaceous Period. It was relatively small, being approximately 6 ft (1.8 m) long, similar to Deinonychus in appearance, with a lethal curved claw on the second toe of each three-toed foot.

(Continued on next page)

Prehistoric *(continued)*

vertebrate	Having a backbone or spinal column.
wing	Either of the two forelimbs of most birds.

Safari

adventure An exciting or very unusual experience.

Africa A continent South of Europe and between the Atlantic and Indian oceans.

Amazon A river in South America. The largest river in the world in terms of volume of water.

armadillo A burrowing, mostly nocturnal mammal, having strong claws and a protective covering of bony plates.

baboon Any of various large monkeys of Africa and Arabia, having a doglike muzzle, large cheek pouches, and a short tail.

binoculars An optical device used to see in the distance, for use with both eyes, consisting of two small telescopes fitted together side by side.

bush A large area thickly covered with a variety of plant growth, trees, etc., as a jungle.

(Continued on next page)

Safari *(continued)*

camel	A large, domesticated mammal with one or two humps on its back and a long neck.
camouflage	The act of hiding by some means that alters or obscures the appearance.
camp	A place where a group of persons or an individual is lodged in a tent or tents or other temporary means of shelter.
canopy	The upper parts of the trees. Home to many creatures including insects, birds, small mammals, and reptiles.
canteen	A small container used for carrying water or other liquids.
carrion	Dead, decaying flesh.
cheetah	A cat, of southwestern Asia and Africa, resembling a leopard but having certain doglike characteristics and great speed.
claw	A sharp, curved nail at the end of a toe of a mammal, reptile, or bird.

(Continued on next page)

Safari *(continued)*

conservation The act of conserving; prevention of injury, decay, waste, or loss; preservation.

desert A region so arid because of little rainfall that it supports only sparse vegetation or no vegetation at all.

elephant A large mammal, characterized by a long trunk, large flapping ears, and ivory tusks.

emergent A giant tree that is much higher than the average canopy height. It houses many birds and insects.

endangered Threatened with extinction.

environment The air, water, minerals, organisms, and all other external factors surrounding and affecting a given organism at any time.

equator The imaginary circle around the earth that is equidistant from the North Pole and South Pole.

expedition A journey or voyage made for a specific purpose.

(Continued on next page)

Safari *(continued)*

fly To move through the air using wings. Also, any of numerous two-winged insects such as the common housefly.

fruit The edible part of a plant developed from a flower.

game Wild animals, including birds and fishes, hunted for food or taken for sport or profit.

gazelle Any small antelope of Africa and Asia, noted for graceful movements and lustrous eyes.

giraffe A tall, long-necked mammal of Africa.

gorilla The largest and most powerful of the apes.

grass A plant having jointed stems, long, thin leaves, and seedlike grains; pasture for grazing animals.

graze To feed on growing grass.

herd A number of animals feeding or traveling together.

(Continued on next page)

Safari *(continued)*

hide	To conceal from sight; also the pelt or skin of one of the larger animals.
hippopotamus	A large plant-eating mammal found in or near the rivers of Africa, having a thick body, short legs, and a large head and muzzle, and able to remain under water for a considerable length of time.
howl	To utter a loud, prolonged, mournful cry.
hunt	To chase or search for, usually for the purpose of catching or killing.
hunter	One who hunts.
hyena	A doglike carnivore of Africa and Asia, having a coarse coat, a sloping back, and large teeth, feeding chiefly on carrion, often in packs.
jeep	A small, rugged motor vehicle.
journey	A traveling from one place to another.
jump	To spring clear of the ground or other support by a sudden muscular effort; leap.

(Continued on next page)

Safari *(continued)*

jungle	A wild land overgrown with dense vegetation, often nearly impenetrable, especially tropical vegetation or a tropical rainforest.
leap	To spring through the air from one point or position to another; jump.
leopard	A large, spotted cat, usually tawny with black markings; panther.
lion	A large, usually tawny-yellow cat native to Africa and southern Asia.
lizard	Any of a group of slender, scaly reptiles with four legs and a tail.
malaria	A disease characterized by chills, fever, and sweating; transmitted to humans when bitten by infected mosquitoes.
migration	A group of animals moving together from one place to another.
mosquito	An insect, the females of which suck the blood of animals and humans, sometimes transmitting disease.

(Continued on next page)

Safari *(continued)*

mountain A natural elevation of the earth's surface having considerable mass, steep sides and a height greater than a hill.

native Being the place in which a person or creature was born or a plant grown; an original inhabitant.

nut A dry fruit consisting of an edible kernel or meat enclosed in a woody or leathery shell.

orangutan A large, long-armed ape with reddish-brown hair.

parasite An organism that lives on or within another.

paw The foot of an animal having claws.

plain An area of flat land not higher than surrounding areas and very little variation in elevation.

poacher A person who trespasses on private property to catch fish or game illegally.

pounce To spring suddenly with the intent to catch or grab something.

(Continued on next page)

Safari *(continued)*

predator	Any organism that exists by preying upon other organisms.
prey	An organism hunted or seized for food.
provisions	A stock of necessary food or supplies.
pygmy	A member of a small-statured people native to Africa.
rain	Water that is condensed from the vapor in the atmosphere and falls to earth in drops.
reptile	Any cold-blooded vertebrate such as turtles, snakes, lizards, crocodiles, etc.
rhinoceros	A large, thick-skinned mammal of Africa and India, having one or more horns on the snout.
rifle	A shoulder firearm.
river	A natural stream of water of fairly large size flowing in a definite course.
riverbed	The channel in which a river flows or used to flow.

(Continued on next page)

Safari *(continued)*

roar	To utter a loud, deep cry or howl.
safari	A journey or expedition, for hunting or exploration.
savanna	A plain characterized by grasses and scattered tree growth.
Serengeti	A plain in Tanzania, including a major wildlife reserve.
sloth	A slow-moving, tree-dwelling South American mammal that hangs from branches.
snake	A limbless, scaly, elongated reptile that may or may not be venomous.
stalk	To pursue or approach prey stealthily.
tail	The hindmost part of an animal.
tent	A portable shelter of skins, canvas, plastic, or other material supported by one or more poles or a frame and often secured by ropes fastened to pegs in the ground.
territory	The area that an animal considers home and defends.

(Continued on next page)

Safari *(continued)*

tracker	One who follows or pursues the tracks, traces, or footprints of another.
trek	To travel or migrate, especially slowly or with difficulty.
tribe	A group of people united by ancestors, customs, and traditions.
trunk	The long nose of an elephant.
tusk	A very long tooth, usually one of a pair, as in the elephant.
water	A transparent, odorless, tasteless liquid that constitutes rain, oceans, lakes, rivers, etc.
watering hole	A pool of water where animals come to drink.
wild	Living in a state of nature; not tamed.
wildebeest	A large African antelope.
yellow fever	An infectious, often fatal disease, caused by a virus transmitted by a mosquito.

(Continued on next page)

Safari *(continued)*

zebra	A horselike African mammal characterized by a pattern of black or brown stripes on a whitish hide.
Zulu	A member of a tribe of people living mainly in South Africa.

Scary / Ghost

abomination A vile, shameful, or detestable action, condition, habit, etc.

apparition A supernatural appearance of a person or thing, especially a ghost.

bat A flying mammal found worldwide, having modified forelimbs that serve as wings and are covered with membranous skin extending to the hind limbs.

black cat A small, domesticated carnivore. Black cats are symbolically associated with witchcraft or evil. Superstition says black cats bring bad luck.

blood The fluid that circulates in the vascular system of human beings and other vertebrates.

bone One of the parts of hard tissue composing the skeleton of most vertebrates.

burial The act or ceremony of burying.

cemetery An area containing graves, tombs, or funeral urns; burial ground; graveyard.

(Continued on next page)

Scary / Ghost *(continued)*

clairvoyant	Having or claiming to have the power of seeing objects or actions beyond the range of natural vision. Also, a person who has these powers.
claw	A sharp, curved nail at the end of a toe of a mammal, reptile, or bird.
coffin	The box or case in which the body of a dead person is placed for burial; casket.
conjure	To produce by or as if by magic or spell.
corpse	A dead body, usually of a human being.
creature	An animal or nonhuman.
crypt	An underground chamber or vault, especially one beneath the main floor of a church, used as a burial place.
darkness	The state or quality of being dark; without light.
death	The act of dying; the end of life.
demise	Death.

(Continued on next page)

Scary / Ghost *(continued)*

demon An evil spirit; devil or fiend.

devil The supreme spirit of evil; Satan; Beelzebub.

doom Unavoidable ill fortune.

doppelganger A ghostly double of a living person.

Dracula Count Dracula, the central character in the novel by Bram Stoker. The most famous of all vampires.

entity Being or existence.

evil Morally wrong or bad; wicked.

experiment An act or operation for the purpose of discovering something unknown or of testing a principle.

fang A long, sharp, hollow or grooved tooth.

fatal Causing or capable of causing death; mortal; deadly.

fear A distressing emotion aroused by impending danger, evil, pain, etc., whether the threat is real or imagined; the feeling or condition of being afraid.

(Continued on next page)

Scary / Ghost *(continued)*

fiend	A diabolically cruel or wicked person.
Frankenstein	A person who creates a monster. Also, Frankenstein the monster and Dr. Frankenstein: the characters in Mary Shelley's novel.
freak	Any abnormal phenomenon or unusual object.
fright	A sudden and extreme fear; a sudden terror.
gargoyle	A grotesquely carved figure of a human or animal.
ghost	The soul of a dead person; a disembodied spirit usually appearing as a shadowy or glowing form; spirit; specter; spook.
ghoul	An evil demon; a grave robber; a person who revels in what is revolting.
goblin	A grotesque sprite or elf that is mischievous or malicious toward people.
grave	A hole in the ground used to bury a dead body.

(Continued on next page)

Scary / Ghost *(continued)*

graveyard	A burial ground; cemetery.
Grim Reaper	The personification of death as a man or cloaked skeleton holding a scythe.
haunt	To visit continually or appear frequently as a spirit or ghost.
haunted house	A residence where spirits or ghosts frequently appear or visit.
horror	An overwhelming and painful feeling caused by something frightfully shocking, terrifying, or revolting.
laboratory	A place equipped to conduct scientific experiments, tests, investigations, etc.
levitate	To rise or float in the air, especially as a result of a supernatural power.
lycanthrope	A werewolf or alien spirit in the physical form of a bloodthirsty wolf.
midnight	The middle of the night; twelve o'clock at night; 12:00 am.
monstrosity	Someone or something monstrous.

(Continued on next page)

Scary / Ghost *(continued)*

mummy	The dead body of a human being or animal preserved by the ancient Egyptian process or a similar method of embalming.
murder	The killing of another human being.
necromancy	A method of telling the future through communication with the dead; black art.
nightmare	A terrifying dream.
Nosferatu	A hideously ugly vampire.
panic	A sudden overwhelming fear that produces hysterical or irrational behavior, and that often spreads quickly through a group of persons or animals.
paranormal	Relating to an occurrence of an event or perception without scientific explanation. Examples: extrasensory perception, telekinesis, and other supernatural phenomena.
phantom	An apparition or specter.
poison	A substance that destroys life or impairs health, usually eaten or swallowed.

(Continued on next page)

Scary / Ghost *(continued)*

poltergeist	A ghost or spirit supposed to manifest its presence by noises, knockings, etc.
potion	A drink having or said to have medicinal, poisonous, or magical powers.
radioactive	Exhibiting radioactivity.
raven	Any of several large birds having shiny, black feathers and a loud, harsh call.
scream	To utter a loud, sharp, piercing cry.
séance	A meeting in which a person attempts to communicate with the spirits of the dead.
shock	A sudden and violent disturbance of the mind or emotions. Also, the physiological effect produced by the passage of an electric current through the body.
shriek	A loud, sharp, shrill cry.
silver bullet	A bullet crafted from pure silver, said to kill a werewolf.

(Continued on next page)

Scary / Ghost *(continued)*

sinister Threatening or suggesting evil, harm, or trouble.

skeleton The bones of a human or an animal considered as a whole.

skull The bony framework of the head, enclosing the brain and supporting the face.

specter A visible spirit, especially one of a terrifying nature; ghost; phantom; apparition.

spell A word, phrase, or form of words supposed to have magic power; charm; incantation.

spirit A supernatural being, especially one inhabiting a place or object.

stake A pointed stick said to kill a vampire when driven through its heart.

supernatural Unexplainable by natural law or phenomena.

terror Intense, sharp fear.

terrify To fill with terror or alarm; make greatly afraid.

(Continued on next page)

Scary / Ghost *(continued)*

tomb An excavation in earth or rock for the burial of a corpse; grave; mausoleum; burial chamber.

tombstone A stone marker on a tomb or grave.

toxic Affected with, or caused by a toxin or poison.

trance A half-conscious state, seemingly between sleeping and waking, in which ability to function voluntarily may be suspended.

vampire A preternatural being, commonly believed to be a reanimated corpse, that sucks the blood of warm-blooded creatures at night.

Van Helsing Dr. Abraham Van Helsing is a fictional character from the novel, Dracula. He is a famous monster hunter and the arch-enemy of Count Dracula.

warlock A man who practices magic; a male witch; sorcerer.

(Continued on next page)

Scary / Ghost *(continued)*

werewolf	According to folklore: a human being who has changed into a wolf, or is capable of assuming the form of a wolf.
witch	A woman who practices magic; sorceress.
witch doctor	A person in some societies who attempts to cure sickness and exorcise evil spirits by the use of magic.
witching hour	According to folklore, the time when supernatural creatures such as witches, demons and ghosts are thought to be at their most powerful, and black magic at its most effective. This hour is typically midnight, but it can also refer to the period from midnight to 3:00 am.
zombie	The body of a dead person given the appearance of life through supernatural powers, usually created for some evil purpose; also called the undead.

Space

alien A creature from outer space; an extraterrestrial.

asteroid A small body composed of rock and metal in orbit about the sun.

astronomy The scientific study of celestial objects and phenomena.

aurora A natural light display in the sky, usually observed at night, particularly in the polar regions.

big bang The theory of a cosmic explosion that began the expansion of the universe.

binary star A system consisting of two stars orbiting around a common center of mass.

black hole A region of space resulting from the collapse of a star, with a gravitational field so strong that not even light can escape it.

celestial Pertaining to the sky or heavens.

comet A small body composed of ice and rock in orbit about the sun.

(Continued on next page)

Space *(continued)*

corona	A colored or white circle seen around a luminous celestial body such as a sun or moon.
crater	A depression formed on the surface of a planet or other celestial body by the impact of a meteorite.
dwarf planet	A celestial body orbiting the sun that is massive enough to have its own gravity but which has not cleared the neighborhood around its orbit and is not a satellite.
Earth	Planet 3rd closest to the sun. The planet we live on.
eclipse	An event in which one celestial object moves into the shadow of another.
exoplanet	A planet outside of the solar system, orbiting another star.
galactic	Pertaining to a galaxy.
galaxy	Any of the billions of systems of stars, gas, and dust that make up the universe.

(Continued on next page)

Space *(continued)*

geostationary	A geosynchronous orbit in which a satellite travels at the appropriate speed and altitude to remain in the same spot above the earth.
geosynchronous	A direct, circular, low inclination orbit about Earth having a period of 23 hours 56 minutes 4 seconds.
globular cluster	An accumulation of stars that orbits around a galactic core.
gravitation	The mutual attraction of all masses in the universe.
gravity	The force of attraction by which items tend to fall toward Earth's center.
interstellar	Between the stars.
Jovian planet	Jupiter-like planets, the gas giants Jupiter, Saturn, Uranus, and Neptune.
Jupiter	Planet 5th closest to the sun. The largest planet in our solar system.
light year	The distance light travels in a year (approximately 5.88 trillion miles or 9.46 trillion kilometers).

(Continued on next page)

Space *(continued)*

luminous	Radiating or reflecting light.
Mars	Planet 4th closest to the sun. Known as the red planet.
Mercury	Planet closest to the sun. The smallest planet in our solar system.
meteor	A meteoroid which is entering Earth's atmosphere from space; called a meteorite after landing.
meteoroid	A small rock in space.
Milky Way	The galaxy which includes the sun and planets of our solar system.
molecular cloud	A large, dense cloud of gas and dust from which new stars are formed.
moon	A small natural body which orbits a larger one; a natural satellite. Also, Moon: the Earth's natural satellite.
nebula	An interstellar cloud of dust and gas.
Neptune	Planet 8th closest to the sun. Known for its dark spot and many moons.
open cluster	A group of up to several thousand young stars held together by mutual gravitation.

(Continued on next page)

Space *(continued)*

orbit	The path of one object around a point or another object.
photosphere	The visible surface of the sun.
Pluto	Dwarf planet; formerly considered the planet farthest from the sun.
red dwarf	A small star, on the order of 100 times the mass of Jupiter.
satellite	A small object or body which orbits a larger one, such as a moon orbiting a planet.
Saturn	Planet 6th closest to the sun. Known for its rings.
solar	Pertaining to the sun.
solar flare	A sudden eruption of hydrogen gas on the sun's surface.
solar system	A sun and all the planets and other bodies that revolve around it.
space shuttle	The spacecraft currently used by the United States government for its human spaceflight missions.
space station	A large structure designed to support human life in space.

(Continued on next page)

Space (continued)

speed of light	The speed at which light travels. Equal to 186,000 miles per second (299,792,458 meters/second).
star	A large, self-luminous, heavenly body such as the sun.
stellar	Pertaining to the stars.
sun	A star that is the central body of a solar system.
supernova	The explosion of a star.
satellite	A small object or body which orbits a larger one, such as a moon orbiting a planet.
universe	The totality of objects and phenomenon throughout space; the cosmos.
Uranus	Planet 7th closest to the sun. Known as the planet that spins on its side.
Venus	Planet 2nd closest to the sun. The brightest planet.
worm hole	A theoretical passageway in space that would link one location or time with another.

Western/Pioneer

ambush A military tactic in which an ambushing force uses concealment, such as brush or large boulders, to attack an enemy that passes its position.

ammunition A generic term meaning a projectile and its propellant; often referred to as ammo.

bandit An outlaw; a bad guy. Also: bandito (Spanish).

barkeep Bartender.

barn A building for storing hay, grain, etc., and often for housing livestock.

beau A male sweetheart.

Black Bart Charles E. Bolles, a California stagecoach robber born in 1829.

blacksmith A person who makes horseshoes and/or forges iron.

bonnet A woman's or child's hat, usually tying under the chin and often framing the face.

(Continued on next page)

Western / Pioneer *(continued)*

boots — Protective footgear, typically leather, covering the foot and part of the leg.

bounty — A reward, especially one offered by the government.

brand — A mark indicating identity or ownership, burned on the hide of an animal with a hot iron.

buck shot — A large lead shot used for shooting deer and other large game.

buckskin — A soft leather made from the skin of a deer.

buffalo chips — A piece of dried cow/steer dung (otherwise known as cow/steer poop).

bull — A male of the cattle family.

calf — A young cow, steer, or buffalo.

cattle — A group of cow or steer.

(Continued on next page)

Western / Pioneer *(continued)*

chaps	A pair of joined leather leggings worn over trousers, especially by cowboys, as protection against burs, rope burns, etc., while on horseback.
chuck wagon	A wagon carrying cooking gear and food for serving people working outdoors, as at a ranch or camp.
claim	A piece of public land which will be used for mining. Miners would "stake a claim" by marking a piece of land with stakes.
colt	A young male horse.
corral	An enclosure or pen for horses, cattle, etc.
covered wagon	A large wagon with a high, bonnetlike canvas top, used by pioneers to transport themselves and their possessions across the North American plains.

(Continued on next page)

Western / Pioneer *(continued)*

cow pie	A small rounded pile of cow dung (otherwise known as cow poop).
cowboy	A man who herds and tends cattle on a ranch, and who traditionally does most of his work on horseback.
deputy	A deputy sheriff; a law-enforcement officer who works for a sheriff.
filly	A young female horse.
foal	A young horse or mule.
forty-niner	A prospector who went to California in 1849 during the gold rush.
frontier	The land or territory that forms the furthest extent of a country's settled or inhabited regions.
general store	A store that sells a wide variety of goods.
genteel	Belonging or suited to polite society; well-bred; refined; elegant; stylish.

(Continued on next page)

Western / Pioneer *(continued)*

ghost town	A town permanently abandoned by its inhabitants.
gold rush	A large scale and hasty movement of people to a region where gold has been discovered, as to California in 1849.
grits	Coarsely ground grain, usually corn, boiled and served for breakfast or as a side dish for meat.
grub	Slang for food.
gun barrel	The tube of a gun through which a bullet travels.
gunslinger	A gunfighter.
hanging judge	A term for a judge who has a reputation for handing out sentences of death by hanging or other harsh methods.
hangman's noose	The rope tied in a closed loop used in hanging condemned prisoners.

(Continued on next page)

Western / Pioneer *(continued)*

hay	Grass that has been cut, dried, stored, and used for animal feed, particularly for grazing animals like cattle, horses, goats, and sheep.
heifer	A young female cow before she has had her first calf.
highway men	Robbers who traveled on horseback.
holster	A carrying case for a gun, attached to a belt, shoulder sling, or saddle.
homestead	A dwelling with its land and buildings occupied as a home.
hoof	The foot of a horse, donkey, or ox.
horse	A large, four-legged plant-eating animal used for carrying or pulling loads and for riding.
horse wrangler	A cowboy who cares for saddle horses.
Indian	An American Indian or Native American.

(Continued on next page)

Western / Pioneer *(continued)*

jail	Prison.
johnny cake	A corn bread made from corn meal and water or milk, prepared on a griddle.
land grant	Land given to an individual or group by the government.
lawman	An officer of the law, such as a sheriff.
livery stable	A stable where horses and vehicles are cared for or rented out for pay.
livestock	The horses, cattle, sheep, and other useful animals kept or raised on a farm or ranch.
log cabin	A cabin made out of logs.
lynch mob	A mob that kills a person for some presumed offense without legal authority.
lynching	An execution without due process of law, typically by hanging, often by a mob.
manure	Dung (otherwise known as poop).

(Continued on next page)

Western / Pioneer *(continued)*

mare	A fully mature female horse.
medicine man	A healer, or someone said to possess supernatural powers (especially among Native Americans).
mill	A building equipped with machinery for grinding grain into flour.
moccasin	A shoe made of soft leather, such as deerskin, worn by Native Americans.
mustang	A small, hardy horse of the American plains.
Oregon Trail	A route used during the westward migration in the U.S., especially between 1840 and 1860, starting in Missouri and ending in Oregon.
outhouse	An outdoor toilet.
outlaw	A criminal, especially one who is a fugitive from the law.
ox	A male animal (cow) used primarily for labor. Plural: oxen.

(Continued on next page)

Western / Pioneer *(continued)*

papoose	An Indian baby or small child.
parlor	A living room; a room in the home used for the reception and entertainment of visitors.
petticoat	A full, ruffled underskirt worn by women.
pioneer	A person who is among the first to settle a region (such as the American West).
pistol	A hand-held gun.
pocket-watch	A watch that is carried in a small watch pocket, often on a long chain.
Pony Express	A system formerly used in the American West to carry mail and packages by relays of riders mounted on ponies.
prairie	A large area of flat or rolling land, with fertile soil, usually treeless, but covered in tall grasses.
prospect	Search for mineral deposits, such as gold.

(Continued on next page)

Western / Pioneer *(continued)*

prospector A person who searches for minerals, such as gold.

provisions A stock of supplies, especially food.

ration A fixed allowance of provisions, especially during a shortage.

rein A narrow leather strap attached in pairs to the bit of a bridle and used by a rider to control a horse.

rifle A shoulder firearm, with a long barrel.

round up To gather a collection of scattered animals.

rustler A cattle thief.

saddle A seat for a rider of a horse or similar animal.

saddlebags A pair of large bags or pouches hung from a saddle or laid over the back of a horse behind the saddle.

(Continued on next page)

Western / Pioneer *(continued)*

sagebrush A low shrub, which covers vast areas of the dry American plains.

saloon A bar; a place where alcoholic drinks are sold and consumed.

schoolhouse A building used as a school, usually with one large room and a single teacher for all the students, regardless of age or grade.

sheriff A law-enforcement officer.

six-shooter A revolver from which six shots can be fired without reloading.

spittoon A bowl, usually made of metal, into which tobacco chewers spit.

spurs Spiked wheels attached to the heels of a horse-rider's boots, used to urge a horse forward.

stagecoach A horse-drawn coach used to carry passengers over a fixed route.

stallion A male horse used for breeding.

(Continued on next page)

Western / Pioneer *(continued)*

steer	A male cow, especially one raised for beef.
stockade	A prison for military personnel; a defense barrier made of strong posts or timbers upright in the ground.
Sutter's Fort	The first non-Native American community in the California Central Valley, founded by John Sutter, and associated with the Donner Party, the California Gold Rush, and the establishment of Sacramento.
tallow	The melted fat from animals used to make candles, soaps, and other products.
telegram	A message sent by telegraph.
telegraph	A system that sends electric impulses along wires to communicate messages across great distances.
tombstone	A stone marker on a tomb or grave.

(Continued on next page)

Western / Pioneer *(continued)*

trading post	A store set up by traders or trading companies to exchange furs or local products for food and supplies.
trail	A path or track made across a wild region or over rough country, made by the passage of people and/or animals.
Transcontinental Railroad	A train route across the United States built by Union Pacific Railroad from the East and Central Pacific Railroad from the West. It was completed in 1869 when the two lines joined in Utah.
trough	A long, narrow wooden box used to hold food or water for animals.
tumbleweed	A plant whose branching upper parts become detached from the roots and are blown by the wind.
vigilante	A person who takes the law into his or her own hands, often to avenge a crime.

(Continued on next page)

Western / Pioneer *(continued)*

wagon train	A caravan of wagons and horses, transporting settlers and/or supplies.
wampum	Beads made from shells used by Indians as a form of money.
whiskey	An alcoholic liquor distilled from a fermented mash of grain such as barley, rye, or corn.
whittle	To trim or shape a stick or piece of wood by carving off pieces with a knife.
Winchester	A rifle, first made in about 1866.

Part III: Better Words

On the pages that follow, you'll find a collection of overly simple, plain words. We call these "jail words." Instead of using these, use one of the suggested replacement words, which are more descriptive, more detailed, or have a special connotation (meaning).

NOTE: You should not use a word whose meaning you do not understand. Be sure to use a dictionary to look up the definitions of any words you do not already know.

NOTE: There are times when using these "jail words" is acceptable. For example, if you are writing a story about a young child or an uneducated person, you should use the words that the character would use in his or her dialogue. Talk with your teacher if you are unsure of which word(s) to use.

Better Words

bad

not good in any manner or degree

Better

awful	extremely bad; unpleasant
beastly	nasty; unpleasant; disagreeable
horrible	causing or tending to cause horror
lousy	mean; miserable
terrible	extremely bad; horrible

Even Better

abominable	repugnantly hateful; detestable; loathsome
atrocious	extremely or shockingly wicked, cruel, or brutal
disastrous	causing great distress or injury; very unfortunate
dreadful	causing great dread, fear, or terror; terrible

Also

corrupt, **disobedient**, **evil**, **naughty**, **vicious**, **vile**, **wicked**, **wretched**

beautiful

having qualities that give satisfaction or great pleasure to see, hear, think about; delighting the senses or mind

Better

gorgeous	splendid or sumptuous in appearance; magnificent
handsome	having a well-proportioned, attractive appearance suggestive of health and strength

Even Better

alluring	very attractive or tempting
dazzling	amazingly impressive
elegant	tastefully fine or luxurious
enticing	highly attractive; arousing hope or desire
exquisite	of special beauty or charm
magnificent	of exceptional beauty, size, etc.
radiant	emitting rays of light; bright with joy
stunning	of striking beauty or excellence

Also

angelic, **appealing**, **beauteous**, **bewitching**, **charming**, **classy**, **comely**, **cute**, **delightful**, **divine**, **enchanting**, **grand**, **lovely**, **pleasing**, **ravishing**, **resplendent**, **splendid**, **superb**

big

large in size, height, width, or amount

Better

enormous	extremely large; much bigger than the common size
giant	having great mass; being huge and bulky
huge	extraordinarily large in extent or quantity
mammoth	immensely large; enormous
mighty	huge; having or showing superior power or strength
monster	huge; ugly or monstrous, frightening

Even Better

burly	having a large body; stout; sturdy
colossal	extremely large
humungous	extremely large
immense	vast; immeasurable; boundless
massive	large and heavy-looking; bulky and heavy
towering	very high or tall

Also

ample, **bulky**, **gargantuan**, **gigantic**, **hefty**, **mega**, **monstrous**, **oversized**, **prodigious**, **spacious**, **stupendous**, **titanic**, **tremendous**, **vast**, **voluminous**, **whopper**, **whopping**

child

a person between birth and full growth, usually between ages three and twelve; often used to identify a relationship to particular parents

Better

baby	a very young child
infant	a child in the earliest period of its life
newborn	recently or only just born
teenager	a person in his or her teens (13 - 19)
toddler	a young child between 1 and 3, learning to walk

Even Better

brat	an annoying, spoiled, or impolite child
minor	anyone under legal age (18 or 21)
punk	a troublemaker, a young hoodlum
squirt	someone who is small and insignificant
tot	a small child
tyke	a small child, especially a boy

Also

adolescent, **babe**, **juvenile**, **kid**, **moppet**, **pre-pubescent**, **pre-teen**, **pubescent**, **rug rat**, **small fry**, **teen**, **teenybopper**, **tween**, **whippersnapper**, **youngster**, **youth**

cold

having a low or subnormal temperature

Better

brisk	sharp and stimulating
chilly	mildly cold
cool	moderately cold; neither warm nor cold
crisp	firm and fresh
freezing	extremely or uncomfortably cold
frosted	covered with or having frost
frosty	consisting of or covered with a frost
frozen	congealed by cold; turned into ice
icy	made of, full of, or covered with ice
snowy	abounding in or covered with snow

Even Better

arctic	characteristic of the extremely cold, snowy, windy weather of the North Pole
frigid	very cold in temperature
glacial	bitterly cold
nippy	chilly or cold
numbing	causing numbness

Also

bitter, **bracing** , **cutting**, **invigorating**, **numbing**, **penetrating**, **tepid**, **wintry**

dark

having very little or no light

Better

dim	not bright
gloomy	dark or dim; deeply shaded
murky	dark, gloomy and cheerless
shadowy	resembling a shadow in faintness
shady	darkness caused by the screening of light rays

Even Better

bleak	depressing; dreary
dusky	somewhat dark; having little light
ominous	foreboding; threatening

Also

clouded, **drab**, **dull**, **foggy**, **inky**, **misty**, **nebulous**, **opaque**, **pitchy**, **sooty**

easy

not hard or difficult; requiring no great effort

Better

basic	fundamental; primary; essential
effortless	requiring or involving no effort; displaying no signs of effort
obvious	easily seen or understood; evident; lacking in subtlety
simple	easy to understand, use, or deal with; not complicated
straightforward	direct; not roundabout; proceeding in a straight course

Even Better

elementary	basic; simple; not compound
manageable	something that can be managed; doable
painless	causing little or no pain; requiring little or no hard work

Also

adolescent, **child's play**, **cinch**, **no problem**, **no sweat**, **no trouble**, **picnic**, **piece of cake**, **smooth sailing**, **snap**

far

at a great distance; a long way off

Better

distant	very far or apart in space or time
faraway	far; often used in fables or fairy-tales
in the distance	far

Even Better

isolated	set or placed apart; detached or separated
outlying	lying at a distance from the center or the main body; remote; lying outside the boundary or limit
remote	isolated; very far from "everything else"
secluded	isolated; shut off; kept apart

Also

far and wide, removed

fast

moving or able to move, operate, function, or take effect quickly

Better

quick	fast; done promptly or rapidly
rapid	fast
speedy	fast; characterized by speed

Even Better

brisk	quick and active; lively; sharp and stimulating; abrupt; curt
hasty	fast; hurried
hurried	characterized by doing something in a hurry; hasty
instantaneous	done in an instant; immediate; sudden
nimble	quick and light; moving with ease; agile
spry	active; nimble; agile; energetic; brisk
swift	fast; without delay; prompt

Also

agile, **breakneck**, **hypersonic**, **like crazy**, **like mad**, **mercurial**, **snappy**, **spirited**, **sprightly**

fat

having too much flabby tissue; overweight

Better

chunky	thick; stout; short and thick
heavy	of great weight; hard to lift or carry; not necessarily fat
overweight	weighing more than is considered normal or proper
plump	well filled out or rounded in form; somewhat fleshy or fat
pudgy	short and fat, or short and thick

Even Better

bulging	a rounded projection, bend, or protrusion
burly	large in body size; stout; sturdy
hefty	heavy; weighty; big and strong; powerful; muscular
obese	very fat

Also

ample, **brawny**, **broad**, **bulky**, **corpulent**, **distended**, **fleshy**, **gross**, **heavyset**, **husky**, **inflated**, **oversize**, **paunchy**, **portly**, **potbellied**, **rotund**, **stout**, **stubby**, **swollen**, **tubby**

fun

something that provides mirth or amusement

Better

amusing	to cause mirth, laughter, or the like
delightful	giving great pleasure or delight
exciting	to arouse or stir up the emotions or feelings
pleasant	pleasing, agreeable
thrilling	producing sudden, strong, and deep emotion or excitement

Even Better

captivating	attracting and holding the attention or interest of
entertaining	amusing; diverting
gratifying	giving pleasure to a person or persons
stimulating	rousing the senses

Also

compelling, **diverting**, **engaging**, **engrossing**, **enjoyable**, **humorous**, **lively**, **moving**, **relaxing**, **stimulating**, **stirring**

funny

causing humor or laughter; amusing

Better

amusing	holding the attention of someone pleasantly
laughable	such as to cause laughter
silly	absurd; ridiculous
wacky	crazy; silly

Even Better

absurd	silly; ludicrous
comical	producing laughter; amusing
hilarious	extremely funny
ridiculous	preposterous; laughable
witty	amusingly clever

Also

droll, **eccentric**, **humorous**, **hysterical**, **ironic**, **kooky**, **loony**, **ludicrous**, **mirthful**, **nutty**, **playful**, **riotous**, **side-splitting**

give

to present voluntarily and without expecting compensation

Better

contribute	to give (money, time, knowledge, assistance, etc.)
donate	to give as a gift
grant	to bestow or confer
present	to furnish or endow with a gift

Even Better

bestow	to present as a gift; give
endow	to equip or supply
impart	to make known; tell; relate
provide	to make available; furnish
relinquish	to renounce or surrender

Also

confer, **equip**, **furnish**, **offer**, **supply**

glad

experiencing pleasure, satisfaction or delight

Better

cheerful	full of cheer; in good spirits
delighted	highly pleased
gleeful	full of exultant joy; merry
pleased	satisfied

Even Better

animated	full of life, action or spirit
joyful	full of joy; glad; delighted
joyous	joyful; happy; jubilant
tickled	excited agreeably

Also

beaming, jubilant

good

satisfactory in quality, quantity, or degree

Better

excellent	possessing outstanding quality or superior merit; remarkably good
fantastic	superb; wonderful; remarkable
marvelous	superb; excellent; great
super	very good; first-rate; excellent
superb	admirably fine or excellent
wonderful	excellent; great; marvelous

Even Better

admirable	worthy of admiration; excellent
agreeable	to one's liking; pleasing
exceptional	unusually excellent; superior
gratifying	satisfying; bringing gratification
satisfactory	giving or affording satisfaction; fulfilling all demands or requirements
splendid	grand; superb; gorgeous; magnificent
stupendous	causing amazement; astounding

Also

acceptable, **capital**, **choice**, **commendable**, **congenial**, **deluxe**, **first-class**, **first-rate**, **great**, **honorable**, **neato**, **nice**, **perfect**, **pleasing**, **prime**, **superior**, **valuable**, **virtuous**, **welcome**

happy

having or showing great pleasure or joy

Better

cheerful	full of cheer; in good spirits
chipper	being in good humor and health
delighted	highly pleased
jolly	in good spirits
merry	joyous in disposition or spirit
upbeat	optimistic; happy

Even Better

content	satisfied with what one is or has; not wanting
ecstatic	in a state of ecstasy
elated	very happy or proud
joyful	showing or expressing joy; delighted
mirthful	joyous; jolly; amused or amusing
overjoyed	feeling great joy or delight
tickled	to excite amusement in

Also

blessed, **blissful**, **blithe**, **captivated**, **exultant**, **gleeful**, **gratified**, **intoxicated**, **jubilant**, **mirthful**, **pleased**, **satisfied**, **thrilled**

hard

not easy; requiring great effort

Better

challenging	testing one's ability; stimulating; interesting; thought-provoking
demanding	calling for an intensive effort or attention
difficult	very hard; not easily performed or performed well
tiring	causing tiredness or weariness
tough	very hard, demanding (casual)

Even Better

complex	complicated; involved; intricate
complicated	complex; involved; intricate
exhausting	very tiring; causing exhaustion
intricate	complicated; elaborate; having many interrelated parts
rigorous	severe or harsh; characterized by rigor; requiring precision

Also

arduous, backbreaking, burdensome, distressing, exacting, formidable, Herculean, knotty, laborious, onerous, rough, rugged, serious, severe, strenuous, taxing, uphill battle, wearying

hate

to dislike strongly

Better

disapprove	to think wrong or reprehensible
dislike	to regard with displeasure
resent	to feel or show displeasure or indignation
scorn	open or unqualified contempt

Even Better

abhor	to regard with extreme repugnancy or aversion
despise	to regard with contempt, distaste, disgust
detest	to feel abhorrence of; hate; dislike intensely
loathe	to feel disgust or intense aversion for; abhor

Also

condemn, **denounce**, **disdain**, **repulsed**

hot

having a notably high temperature

Better

broiling	exposing to great heat, as in cooking
fiery	containing fire
roasting	exceedingly hot; scorching
steamy	hot and humid

Even Better

muggy	oppressively humid; damp and close
scalding	causing a burning sensation, as from contact with hot liquid
scorching	burning; very hot
sultry	oppressively hot and close or moist
sweltering	characterized by oppressive heat

Also

boiling, **burning**, **feverish**, **molten**, **piping hot**, **searing**, **sizzling**, **toasty**, **torrid**, **tropical**, **warm**

hurt

to cause injury or pain; injure; damage; harm

Better

damage	reduce the value or usefulness of
harm	hurt; injure; damage
injure	hurt; harm; damage; impair
punish	subject to pain as a penalty
weaken	make weak or weaker
wound	injure in a way that causes tissue rupture

Even Better

abuse	treat in a harmful, offensive way
batter	beat or pound repeatedly
bruise	cause a discolored spot on the skin; cause damage to a person's ego
cripple	disable; impair; weaken; make a cripple of
torture	inflict excruciating pain; cause extreme anguish

Also

impair, **maim**, **mangle**, **mar**

interesting

engaging or exciting and holding the attention or curiosity

Better

exciting	producing excitement; thrilling
fascinating	of great interest or attraction

Even Better

captivating	attracting and holding the attention or interest of, as by beauty or excellence
compelling	having a powerful, irresistible effect
engaging	winning; attractive; pleasing
engrossing	fully occupying the mind or attention
entertaining	affording entertainment; amusing
gripping	holding the attention or interest intensely
intriguing	arousing the curiosity of interest of by unusual, new or compelling qualities
stimulating	rousing or quickening activity or the senses
thrilling	producing sudden and strong emotion or excitement

Also

absorbing, **affecting**, **alluring**, **amusing**, **attractive**, **charismatic**, **curious**, **delightful**, **enchanting**, **enthralling**, **entrancing**, **exceptional**, **magnetic**, **pleasurable**, **provocative**, **refreshing**, **riveting**, **stirring**, **striking**, **thought-provoking**

light (brightness)

giving off or reflecting much light

Better

blinding	so bright as to deprive one of sight
bright	radiating or reflecting light
glaring	shining with or reflecting a harshly bright or brilliant light
glittering	sparkling brilliantly; glistening
shiny	bright or glossy in appearance
sparkling	shining or glistening with gleams of light
sunny	abounding in sunshine
twinkling	shining with intermittent gleams of light

Even Better

dazzling	shining or reflecting brilliantly
illuminated	brightened with light
luminous	radiating or reflecting light
lustrous	having luster; shining; luminous

Also

agleam, **aglitter**, **beaming**, **bedazzling**, **brilliant**, **flashing**, **flickering**, **gleaming**, **glimmering**, **glinting**, **glistening**, **glowing**, **incandescent**, **lucent**, **polished**, **radiant**, **shimmering**, **shining**

light (weight)

of little weight; not heavy

Better

delicate	fine in texture or quality; requiring great care
fluffy	light or airy; resembling fluff
thin	not thick; slender; lacking fullness or volume

Even Better

airy	like air; immaterial; light in movement; graceful; delicate
buoyant	tending to float in a fluid manner
flimsy	weak; not strong or solid
portable	capable of being transported; easily carried
sheer	transparently thin

Also

dainty, **downy**, **inconsequential**, **lithe**, **meager**, **slender**, **slight**, **trifling**, **trivial**

little

small in size; not big; not large

Better

dinky	small in size; unimportant; unimpressive
miniature	a representation or image of something on a reduced scale
skimpy	lacking in size, fullness
teeny	exceptionally small
tiny	very small

Even Better

infinitesimal	exceedingly small
microscopic	so small as to be invisible to the naked eye
minute	extremely small, as in size, amount, extent or degree
slight	small in amount, degree
sparse	not thick or dense

Also

elfin, **imperceptible**, **inconsiderable**, **insufficient**, **Lilliputian**, **limited**, **meager**, **miniscule**, **petite**, **pygmy**, **stumpy**, **stunted**, **wee**

look

to turn one's eyes toward something or in some direction in order to see

Better

inspect	view closely and critically
notice	become aware of; perceive; pay attention
stare	look intently, esp. with eyes wide open
watch	look attentively; be on the lookout attentively

Even Better

examine	inspect or scrutinize carefully; investigate
gaze	look steadily and intently, with curiosity, interest, pleasure, or wonder
glance	look quickly or briefly; glimpse
glare	stare with a fierce or angry look
glimpse	look very quickly or briefly; glance
observe	watch or note for a scientific, official, or other special purpose

Also

gawk, **glower**, **leer**, **ogle**, **peek**, **peep**, **scan**, **scrutinize**, **search**, **surveil**, **view**

love

a feeling of strong or constant regard for and dedication to someone

Better

admire	to regard with wonder, pleasure, or approval
adore	to regard with the utmost esteem, love, and respect; honor
cherish	to hold or treat as dear; feel love for
desire	to wish or long for; crave; want
devoted	zealous or ardent in attachment, loyalty, or affection (adj)
fancy	a liking; capricious preference; inclination
relish	pleasurable appreciation of anything; liking

Even Better

idolize	to regard with blinding adoration or devotion
infatuated	inspired or possessed with a foolish or unreasoning passion (adj)
worship	adoring reverence or regard

Also

enamored (adj), **esteem**, **glorify**, **treasure**, **venerate**

mad

greatly provoked or irritated

Better

angry	feeling or showing strong resentment
annoyed	slightly irritated
crabby	grouchy; ill-natured
cranky	grouchy; ill-tempered
furious	full of fury or rage
grumpy	irritable; grouchy

Even Better

berserk	wild; crazed
cross	annoyed
enraged	in a rage; infuriated
irate	angry; enraged
livid	furiously angry; strangulated by strong emotion
peeved	annoyed or irritated
testy	edgy; snappish; irritably impatient; touchy

Also

grouchy, **indignant**, **irritated**, **petulant**, **sarcastic**, **sharp**, **wild**, **wrathful**

mean

offensive, selfish, or ungenerous

Better

awful	inspiring fear
evil	morally wrong or bad
nasty	vicious, spiteful
rotten	wretchedly bad, unpleasant; miserable
rude	impolite

Even Better

cantankerous	disagreeable to deal with
despicable	deserving to be despised
dreadful	causing great dread or fear
malicious	full of malice; spiteful
savage	ferocious or cruel
snide	derogatory in a nasty manner
vicious	readily disposed to evil

Also

bad-tempered, **callous**, **churlish**, **contemptible**, **disagreeable**, **hard**, **infamous**, **pesky**, **scurrilous**

nice

considerate and helpful; of a good or benevolent nature

Better

charming	pleasing; delightful
friendly	showing friendship; like a friend
generous	giving or sharing a lot; unselfish
gentle	mild; not rough, severe, or violent
helpful	giving aid or assistance; useful; beneficial
kind	nice; considerate and helpful
polite	showing good manners; courteous

Even Better

considerate	showing kindly awareness or regard for another's feelings
courteous	having or showing good manners; polite
delightful	giving great pleasure or delight
gracious	pleasant; kind; courteous; characterized by good taste, comfort, ease, or luxury

Also

affectionate, **agreeable**, **altruistic**, **amiable**, **benevolent**, **charitable**, **commendable**, **compassionate**, **cordial**, **cultured**, **genial**, **kind-hearted**, **kindly**, **lovely**, **philanthropic**, **pleasant**, **sweet**, **swell**, **well-mannered**

old

far advanced in the years of life

Better

aged	having lived or existed long
ancient	of times long past
elderly	somewhat old; near old age
mature	fully developed in body and mind; full grown
senior	one who is older, of higher rank; elder

Even Better

decrepit	weakened by old age; worn out
doddering	shaky or trembling, as from old age
fossil	a markedly outdated or old-fashioned person or thing
infirm	feeble or weak in body or health, especially because of age
venerable	commanding respect because of great age

Also

debilitated, **enfeebled**, **geriatric**, **grizzled**, **seasoned**, **senile**

pretty

pleasing or attractive to the eye

Better

beautiful	wonderful; very pleasing or satisfying
cute	pretty, especially in a dainty way; precious

Even Better

adorable	very attractive or delightful; charming
darling	dearly loved; charming; cute; lovable
elegant	tastefully fine or luxurious in dress, style, etc.
glamorous	charmingly or fascinatingly attractive, especially in a mysterious or magical way
gorgeous	splendid; sumptuous in appearance, etc.; magnificent
lovely	charmingly or exquisitely beautiful; having a beauty that appeals to the heart or mind as well as to the eye
stunning	astonishing; astounding; overwhelming

Also

alluring, **angelic**, **attractive**, **beckoning**, **bewitching**, **captivating**, **comely**, **dainty**, **dazzling**, **delicate**, **divine**, **enchanting**, **exquisite**, **graceful**, **precious**, **radiant**, **ravishing**, **refined**, **tantalizing**

quiet

making little, if any, noise or sound

Better

dumb lacking the power of speech
hushed silent or quiet
muffled wrapped with something to deaden or prevent sound
peaceful free from strife, commotion, or disorder
silent making no sound; still; refraining from speech

Even Better

inaudible incapable of being heard
soundless without sound; silent
speechless temporarily deprived of speech because of strong emotion, physical weakness, or exhaustion
taciturn inclined to silence, reserved in speech
tight-lipped speaking very little; close-mouthed

Also

calm, **lull**, **noiseless**, **reticent**, **secretive**, **still**, **tranquil**, **uncommunicative**

run

to travel on foot more rapidly than at a walk and in such a manner that for an instant in each step all or both feet are off the ground

Better

dash	move suddenly, usually for a short time
fly	move quickly; flee; escape
jog	run at a leisurely, slow pace
race	run fast; often in a contest of speed
rush	go rapidly or suddenly, often impetuously
sprint	run at full speed, esp. for a short distance

Even Better

bolt	run suddenly; escape; flee
dart	move suddenly and abruptly
hustle	run, demonstrating effort; leave roughly
scamper	run playfully, as a child
scurry	move quickly, in haste

Also

bound, **charge**, **escape**, **evade**, **flee**, **gallop**, **lope**, **scamper**, **trot**, **zip**, **zoom**

sad

affected by unhappiness or grief

Better

blue unhappy; glum
depressed sad and gloomy; dejected; downcast
dismal causing gloom or dejection; dreary; cheerless
glum silently gloomy; dejected

Even Better

bereaved greatly saddened by the death of a loved one
bitter marked by strong resentment or cynicism
dejected depressed in spirits; disheartened
despondent feeling or showing profound hopelessness
forlorn desolate or dreary; unhappy or miserable
melancholy a gloomy state of mind
sorrowful feeling sorrow; grieved; sad

Also

cheerless, **distressed**, **doleful**, **heart-broken**, **languishing**, **low**, **morbid**, **morose**, **mournful**, **pessimistic**, **sorry**, **troubled**, **woebegone**

short

having relatively little height

Better

dinky	small; unimportant; unimpressive
dumpy	short and stout; squat
dwarfish	like a dwarf, especially in being abnormally small
pint-size	comparatively small in size
squat	low and thick or broad
stubby	of the nature of or resembling a stub

Even Better

diminutive	small; little; tiny
petite	short and having a small, trim figure
slight	slender or slim
stunted	slowed or stopped abnormally in growth or development

Also

impish, **puny**, **tiny**

slow

moving or proceeding with little or less than usual speed

Better

crawling	to move slowly on hands and knees or by dragging the body along the ground
creeping	slow-moving; with the body close to the ground
plodding	proceeding in a tediously slow manner

Even Better

dawdling	moving slowly, languidly; sauntering
gradual	taking place, changing, or moving by small degrees or little by little
idle	not active
leisurely	acting, proceeding, or done without haste; unhurried
listless	having or showing little or no interest in anything
sluggish	lacking in energy; lazy; having little motion

Also

apathetic, **deliberate**, **disinclined**, **inching**, **inert**, **lackadaisical**, **lazy**, **negligent**, **reluctant**, **slothful**, **snail's pace**, **tardy**

small

of limited size; not big; little

Better

cramped	confined or severely limited in space
humble	low in rank, importance, or status
limited	confined within limits; restricted
miniature	a representation or image of something on a reduced scale
petite	short and having a trim figure
slight	small in amount or degree

Even Better

inadequate	not adequate or sufficient; unsuitable
meager	deficient in quantity or quality; lacking fullness or richness
modest	having or showing a modest estimate of one's importance or merits
puny	of less than normal size and strength; weak
runty	stunted; dwarfish
wee	little; very small

Also

bitty, **diminutive**, **inadequate**, **insufficient**, **paltry**, **pint-sized**, **scanty**, **stunted**, **teensy**, **teeny**

smart

having or showing a quickness of mind

Better

bright	quick-witted or intelligent
brilliant	having great intelligence, talent, or quality
educated	characterized by qualities of culture and learning
intelligent	having a high mental capacity
quick	keenly responsive; lively; acute
wise	having the power of discerning and judging properly as to what is true or right

Even Better

clever	having sharp or quick intelligence
creative	having the quality or power of creating
cunning	skill employed in a shrew or sly manner, as in deceiving
ingenious	characterized by cleverness or originality of invention or construction

Also

alert, **astute**, **brainy**, **gifted**, **insightful**, **inventive**, **knowledgeable**, **literate**, **logical**, **perceptive**, **rational**, **sage**, **savvy**, **scholarly**, **schooled**, **sensible**, **sharp**, **shrewd**, **skilled**, **sound**, **wily**

soft

not hard or stiff; yielding readily to touch or pressure

Better

cottony	of or like cotton
cushiony	soft and comfortable
feathery	resembling feathers; light; airy
flimsy	without strength
fluffy	light or airy; resembling fluff
furry	consisting of or resembling fur
silky	of or like silk; smooth; lustrous; delicate
squishy	soft and wet

Even Better

comfortable	producing or affording physical comfort, support, or ease
delicate	fine in texture, quality, or construction; fragile; frail
silken	like silk in smoothness, softness, glossiness, or delicateness

Also

bendable, **comfy**, **cozy**, **doughy**, **downy**, **elastic**, **fine**, **flabby**, **fleecy**, **flowing**, **gelatinous**, **limp**, **malleable**, **moldable**, **mushy**, **pliable**, **satiny**, **smooth**, **spongy**, **squashy**, **supple**, **velvety**, **yielding**

stupid

dumb; unintelligent; dull; foolish; senseless; annoying

Better

brainless	stupid; mentally weak; foolish
foolish	lacking sense, forethought, or caution; insignificant
idiotic	like an idiot; senselessly foolish or stupid
pointless	without a point, meaning, or relevance

Even Better

dense	slow to learn or understand
mindless	senseless; lacking intelligence or good sense
moronic	notably stupid or lacking in good judgment
senseless	nonsensical; meaningless; silly
trivial	of very little importance; insignificant; ordinary

Also

dull, **dumb**, **feebleminded**, **imbecilic**, **insane**, **irritating**, **meaningless**, **obtuse**, **simple**, **simpleminded**, **slow**, **tedious**, **thick**, **troublesome**, **witless**

take

to grasp or grip; to get into one's hands

Better

acquire	to gain for oneself through one's actions or efforts
grab	to seize suddenly or quickly; snatch; to take illegal possession of; to seize forcibly
grasp	to seize and hold by clasping with the fingers or arms
steal	to take without permission or right, especially secretly or by force

Even Better

capture	to take or gain control by force
collect	to gather together; assemble; accumulate
nab	to snatch; to steal
obtain	to come into possession of; acquire through effort or request
seize	to take hold of suddenly or forcibly; to grasp
snatch	to seize; to grasp hastily; to kidnap (slang)

Also

abduct, **bag**, **earn**, **ensnare**, **entrap**, **gather up**, **grip**, **procure**, **reap**, **secure**, **snag**

talk

to communicate or exchange ideas

Better

chat	to talk in a familiar or informal manner
discuss	to talk over; to consider or examine by argument or comment
speak	to deliver an address (more formal)
tell	to give an account or narrative of; relate

Even Better

babble	to utter sounds or words imperfectly, indistinctly, or without meaning (as a baby or crazy person would)
gossip	to discuss rumors, especially about the personal or private affairs of others
inform	to give or impart knowledge; to train
jive	to tease, fool, or kid (slang)
lecture	to instruct or inform; to reprimand
notify	to inform; to give notice

Also

announce, **chatter**, **conference**, **confess**, **converse**, **cry**, **divulge**, **exhort**, **gab**, **harangue**, **jive**, **pronounce**, **rap**, **recite**, **sermonize**, **yak**

tall

extending to a great distance upward

Better

gigantic enormous; immense
steep having an almost vertical slope or pitch
towering very high or tall; lofty

Even Better

formidable causing fear, apprehension, or dread
lofty extending high in the air
majestic characterized by or possessing majesty; of lofty dignity or imposing aspect
statuesque like or suggesting a statue, as in massive or majestic dignity, grace, or beauty

Also

grand, **immense**, **sky-scraping**

thin

having a noticeably small amount of body fat

Better

bony of or like bone; skinny
gaunt extremely thin and bony
lanky ungracefully thin
lean without much flesh or fat
skinny very lean or thin
slender thin or slight; light and graceful
slim slender, as in girth or form; slight in build or structure
wiry lean and sinew

Even Better

anorexic suffering from anorexia nervosa, an eating disorder which causes loss of appetite or inability to eat; pathologically thin
emaciated made abnormally lean or thin by a gradual wasting away of flesh
scrawny excessively thin; lean
skeletal of, pertaining to, or like a skeleton
willowy tall, slender, and moving gracefully

Also

angular, **cadaverous**, **haggard**, **lithe**, **reedy**, **sinewy**, **slight**, **spare**, **spindly**, **twiggy**, **waifish**, **waspish**

tired

exhausted, as by exertion; fatigued or sleepy

Better

beat	very tired
bored	uninterested
drowsy	half-asleep; sleepy
run-down	weary
sleepy	ready or inclined to sleep
weary	physically or mentally exhausted

Even Better

burned-out	consumed; overused to the point of being useless
drained	depleted to the point of complete exhaustion
exhausted	completely worn out
fatigued	weariness from bodily or mental exertion
haggard	having an exhausted appearance, as from prolonged suffering, exertion or anxiety
stale	having lost freshness, vigor, initiative, as from overstrain or boredom

Also

consumed, **distressed**, **dog-tired**, **overtaxed**, **overworked**, **pooped**, **stale**, **tuckered**, **wiped-out**

ugly

unpleasant to look at

Better

frightful	such as to cause fright; dreadful; terrible; alarming
hideous	horrible or frightful to the senses
homely	lacking in physical attractiveness; not beautiful
monstrous	frightful or hideous in appearance; extremely ugly
plain	not beautiful; physically unattractive or undistinguished

Even Better

appalling	causing dismay or horror
grisly	causing a shudder or feeling of horror
gruesome	causing great horror; grisly
loathsome	causing feelings of loathing; disgusting; revolting
repulsive	causing repugnance or aversion
revolting	disgusting; repulsive

Also

deformed, **foul**, **unsightly**, **vile**

walk

to travel on foot at a moderate speed or pace

Better

hike walk a great distance, especially through rural areas

march walk with regular and measured tread; advance in step in an organized body, in a stately, deliberate manner

stroll walk leisurely

Even Better

amble to walk at a slow, easy pace; stroll

stride walk with long steps, as with vigor, haste, impatience, or arrogance

strut walk with a vain, pompous bearing, as with head erect and chest thrown out, as if to impress

wander travel without a fixed purpose or direction

Also

canter, **lumber**, **meander**, **plod**, **roam**, **saunter**, **scuff**, **shuffle**, **slog**, **stalk**, **traipse**, **tramp**, **tread**, **trek**, **trudge**

Part IV: Weak Words

Remove all unnecessary, redundant, and weak words from your writing.

Unnecessary and redundant words slow your readers down. Because these words don't contribute any forward movement or essential information, you are usually better off removing them.

Weak words sap the energy of your writing. They are bland and dull, boring like a limp noodle. Weak words don't add much to your writing. Replace these overused or generic words with words that are shiny and spicy. It's worth it!

Weak Words

thing, stuff

Use more specific, interesting words.

Needs Editing:	Better:
I tried to hit the thing with the thing, but I hit the other thing instead.	I tried to hit the fly with the fly swatter, but I hit the lamp instead.
I got some great stuff for my birthday.	I got a trampoline and a shiny, red bike for my birthday.

Notes

Specific, detailed words entertain and inform better than vague, blah words like these.

very, really, pretty

Use more specific, interesting words. Don't repeat!

Needs Editing:	Better:
The car drove very fast down the street.	The car sped down the street.
I really, really had to go to the bathroom.	I had to go to the bathroom. —OR— I was dying to go to the bathroom. —OR— I had to go to the bathroom. I was tapping my foot and wiggling in order to hold it.
Ned was pretty mad at Ted.	Ned was furious with Ted.

Notes

Specific, detailed words entertain and inform better than vague, blah words, even when you attempt to strengthen them with these weak adjectives.

fun, boring

Use specific, interesting words which give details and *paint a picture.*

Needs Editing:	**Better:**
The party was fun.	Sam's playlist had hours and hours of great dance music. Everyone danced the whole night long. Bobby was a crackup, telling jokes each time we stopped to get a soda.
Needs Editing:	**Better:**
The party was boring.	Sam forgot the CD player, so we didn't have any music. We just stood around, the girls on one side of the room, and the guys on the other. Nobody talked.

Notes

Don't just tell us something was/is fun or boring. Show the details of the situation!

Other weak examples: **fine**, **okay**, **all right**

cool, awesome

Use specific, interesting words which give details and *paint a picture*.

Needs Editing:
Nick is so cool. His house is awesome.

Better:
Nick is always telling jokes or goofing around. The other day, he came to school with a lamp shade on his head! His house is huge, with a play room full of video games and a swimming pool in the backyard.

Notes

Don't just tell us something was/is cool or awesome. Show the details of the situation!

Other weak examples: **amazing**, **great**

many, a lot, lots

Use more specific, interesting words.

Needs Editing:	**Better:**
José has a lot of model trucks.	José has more than 100 model trucks.
Needs Editing:	**Better:**
Cindy has many, many pairs of shoes.	Cindy has a walk-in closet full of shoes.

Notes

Specific, detailed words entertain and inform better than vague, blah words, even when you attempt to strengthen them with these weak adjectives.

then, next

Don't overuse these word when describing steps or instructions.

Needs Editing:

I took out all the ingredients. Then I mixed the batter and the eggs. Then I added the water. Then I added the oil. Then I mixed some more. Then I put butter in the pan. Then I used a spoon to scoop out the batter and dropped it into the pan. Then I flipped the pancakes. Then I took them out of the pan. Then I ate them.

Better:

I started by taking out all the ingredients. Once I was ready, I mixed the batter and the eggs, then added the water and oil and mixed some more. Next I put butter in the pan. I used a spoon to scoop out the batter and dropped it into the pan. After a while, I flipped the pancakes, and after a while longer, I took them out of the pan. Finally, I ate them.

Notes

Mix in other words and phrases. Don't let your writing get monotonous (boring, having no variety).

what happened was

Don't introduce what happened with *what happened was*, *what we did was*, or similar phrases.

Needs Editing:
What I did on my summer vacation was that I went to camp. What happened was that I did arts and crafts and went canoeing. What my favorite part was making flowers out of pipe cleaners.

Better:
I went to camp over summer vacation. I made arts and crafts and went canoeing. My favorite part was making flowers out of pipe cleaners.

Notes

Get right to it! Re-write to remove these phrases.

there is/was/were

Don't introduce what was or what is with the phrases *there is*, *there was*, *there were*, *there are*, *it is*, or *it was*.

Needs Editing:

It is my mother who does the laundry, not me. It is to be expected that kids don't normally do their own laundry. There are some children who do the laundry, but not many. If there are kids in my neighborhood who have to do their family's laundry, I feel sorry for them.

Better:

My mother does the laundry, not me. Kids don't normally do their own laundry. Some children do the laundry, but not many. If any kids in my neighborhood have to do their family's laundry, I feel sorry for them.

Notes

Get right to it! Re-write to remove these phrases.

personally, I think

Don't use these unless there is a chance your reader will confuse your opinion for someone else's.

Needs Editing:	**Better:**
Personally, I think there is too much homework assigned. —OR— I think there is too much homework assigned.	There is too much homework assigned.

Notes

Your readers assume any opinions they read are yours unless you specifically state otherwise.

thought to myself

Don't use *to myself*, *to himself*, or *to herself* when describing someone thinking.

Needs Editing:
I've got to get out of here, Mrs. Clayton thought to herself.

Better:
I've got to get out of here, Mrs. Clayton thought.

Notes

People can't think to anyone but themselves. Don't use these redundant clauses.

Part V: Other Resources

In this section you'll find a collection of useful resources, including:

(continued on next page)

Other Resources *(continued)*

Commonly Misspelled Words

A

a lot
about
absence
abundance
acceptable
accessible
accidentally
acclaim
accommodate
accomplish
accordion
accumulate
achievement
acquaintance
acquire
acquit
acquitted
across
actually
address
advertisement
again
aggravate
all right
alleged
along
already
also
although
always
amateur
amend
amendment
among
analysis
analyze
annual
another
anyone
apartment
apologize
apparatus
apparent
appearance
appropriate
arctic
arguing
argument
arithmetic
ascend
assassinated
atheist
athletic
athletics
attendance
attitude
aunt
author
autumn
auxiliary
awhile

B

balance
balloon
barbecue
bargain
basically
battalion
beautiful
because
been
before
beggar
beginning
belief
believe
beneficial

(continued on next page)

Commonly Misspelled Words *(continued)*

B *(continued)*

benefit
benefited [1]
benefits
birthday
biscuit
blue
bought
bouillon
boundaries
boundary
breakfast
Britain
brought
Buddha
built
business
busy

[1] also: benefitted

C

calendar
camouflage
canceled [2]
candidate
cannot
can't
cantaloupe
capable
Caribbean
category
caught
celebrate
cemetery
chagrined
challenge
changeable
changing
character
characteristic
chief
children
chocolate
climbed
close
cloth
clothes
clothing
collectible
colonel
color
colossal
column
come
coming
commission
commitment
committed
committee
communicate
comparative
compelled
competent
competition
completely
concede

[2] Also: cancelled

(continued on next page)

Commonly Misspelled Words *(continued)*

C *(continued)*

conceivable
conceive
condemn
condescend
conferred
conscience
conscientious
conscious
consciousness
consensus
consistent
contagious
continuous
control
controlled
controversial
controversy
convenient
coolly
corollary
correlate
correspondence
cough
could
counselor
country
courteous
courtesy
cousin
criticism
criticize
crystal
cupboard

D

dairy
dear
deceive
decorate
defendant
deferred
definite
definitely
definition
dependent
descend
describe
description
desirable
despair
desperate
determine
develop
development
dictionary
didn't
difference
different
dilemma
dining
disappearance
disappoint
disaster
disastrous
discipline
disease
dispensable
dissatisfied
doctor
doesn't
dominant
dormitory
dumbbell

Commonly Misspelled Words *(continued)*

E

early
easily
easy
ecstasy
efficiency
eighth
either
elementary
eligible
eliminate
embarrass
embarrassment
emergency
eminent
emperor
encouragement
encouraging
enemy
enough
entirely
environment
equality
equipment
equipped
equivalent
especially
every
everybody
everyone
exaggerate
exceed
excellence
excellent
excitement
exhaust
exhilarate
existence
existent
expense
experience
experiment
explanation
extremely
exuberance

F

facsimile
fallacious
fallacy
familiar
fascinate
fascinating
favorite
feasible
February
fictitious
fiery
finally
financially
first
fluorescent
forcibly
foreign
foresee
forfeit
formerly
forty
fourth
frantically
friends
fruit
fuel
fueling
fulfill
fundamentally

Commonly Misspelled Words *(continued)*

G

gauge
generally
genius
geography
getting
goes
government
governor
grade
grammar
grandeur
grateful
grievous
guarantee
guaranteed
guard
guardian
guerrilla
guess
guidance

H

half
handkerchief
happily
harass
having
hear
heard
height
heinous
hello
hemorrhage
here
heroes
hesitancy
hierarchy
hindrance
hoarse
hoping
hospital
hour
house
humorous
hygiene
hypocrisy
hypocrite

I

ideally
idiosyncrasy
ignorance
imaginary
immediate
immediately
implement
incidentally
incredible
independence
independent
indicted
indispensable
inevitable
influential
information
inoculate
instead
insurance
integrated
intellectual

(continued on next page)

Commonly Misspelled Words *(continued)*

I *(continued)*

intelligence
intercede
interesting
interference
interrupt
introduce
irrelevant
irresistible
island

J

jealousy
jewelry
judgment [3]
judicial
juicy

[3] Also: judgement

K

kernel
knew
know
knowledge

L

laboratory
laid
language
larynx
later
latter
laugh
league
led
legitimate
leisure
length
lenient
lessons
let's
letter
liaison
library
license
lieutenant
lightning
likelihood
likely
literature
little
loneliness
longitude
lovable
lovely
loving
luxury

Commonly Misspelled Words *(continued)*

M

magazine
maintain
maintenance
making
manageable
maneuver
manufacture
many
marriage
mathematics
maybe
mayor
medicine
medieval
memento
mere
might
millennium
millionaire
miniature
minimum
minuscule
minute
minutes
miscellaneous
mischievous
missile
misspell
misspelled
morning
mortgage
mosquito
mosquitoes
mother
mourning
murmur
muscle
museum
mysterious

N

name
narrative
naturally
necessary
necessity
Negroes
neighbor
neither
neutron
nice
ninety
ninth
no one
none
noticeable
nowadays
nuisance

Commonly Misspelled Words *(continued)*

O

obedience
obstacle
occasion
occasionally
occurred
occurrence
o'clock
official
often
omission
omit
omitted
once
one
opinion
opponent
opportunity
oppression
optimism
optimistic
orchestra
ordinarily
origin
original
our
outrageous
outside
overrun

P

paid
pamphlets
panicky
parallel
paralysis
paralyze
parliament
particular
particularly
party
pastime
pavilion
peace
peaceable
peculiar
penetrate
people
perceive
performance
permanent
permissible
permitted
perseverance
persistence
personal
personnel
perspiration
philosophy
physical
physician
picnicking
piece
pilgrimage
pitiful
planning
played
playwright
pleasant
poison
political
portray
possess
possession
possessive
possibility

(continued on next page)

Commonly Misspelled Words *(continued)*

P *(continued)*

possible
potato
potatoes
practically
practice
prairie
precede
precedence
preceding
preference
preferred
prejudice
preparation
prescription
pretty
prevalent
primitive
privilege
probably
procedure
proceed
proceeded
profession
professor
prominent
pronounce
pronunciation
propaganda
psychology
publicity
publicly
purposely
pursue

Q

quandary
quantity
quarantine
quarter
questionnaire
queue
quit
quite
quizzes

R

raise
raspberry
read
realistic
realistically
realize
really
recede
receipt
receive
receiving
recognize
recommend
reference
referred
referring
relevant
relieving
religious
remember
remembrance
reminiscence
repetition
representative
resemblance
reservoir
resistance

(continued on next page)

Commonly Misspelled Words *(continued)*

R *(continued)*

restaurant
rheumatism
rhyme
rhythm
rhythmical
ridiculous
right
roommate
rough
round
route

S

sacrifice
sacrilegious
safety
said
salary
satellite
says
scary
scenery
schedule
school
secede
secretary
seize
sense
sentence
separate
separation
sergeant
several
severely
shepherd
shining
siege
similar
simile
simply
simultaneous
sincerely
skiing
soliloquy
something
soon
sophomore
souvenir
specifically
specimen
sponsor
spontaneous
statistics
statue
stopped
store
straight
strategy
strength
strenuous
stubbornness
studying
subordinate
substitute
subtle
succeed
success
successfully
succession
sufficient
sugar
supersede
suppose
suppress
surely
surprise

(continued on next page)

Commonly Misspelled Words *(continued)*

S *(continued)*

surround
surrounded
survival
susceptible
suspicious
swimming
syllable
symmetrical
synonymous

T

tangible
teacher
tear
technical
technique
temperamental
temperature
tendency
terrible
their
themselves
theories
there
therefore
they're
threshold
tired
together
tomorrow
tonight
tournament
tourniquet
toward
tragedy
transferred
transferring
traveling
tries
trouble
truly
twelfth
tyranny

U

unanimous
undoubtedly
unforgettable
unfortunately
unique
unnecessary
until
usable
usage
used
usual
usually
utilization

Commonly Misspelled Words *(continued)*

V

vacation
vacuum
valuable
vengeance
very
vigilant
village
villain
violence
virtue
visible
vision
volume

W

warrant
warrior
Wednesday
weigh
weird
what
when
wherever
white
who
whole
wholly
withdrawal
woman
women
worthwhile
would
write
writing
wrote

Y

yacht
yield
young

Commonly Misused Words

Here is a list of commonly misused words and phrases. Use this list to help you choose the proper words and/or phrases.

A / An

I have a banana. You have an apple. I want a unicorn. You want an hour to play video games.

Use *a* before words that begin with a consonant sound. Use *an* before words that begin with a vowel sound. Note that it is the first *sound* that matters, not the first *letter*.

Accept / Except

Sam hopes Eve will accept his request to go to the dance. Everyone is going to the dance except Barney.

The word *accept* means to receive. The word *except* means to exclude or to leave out.

Adapt / Adopt

It is amazing how dogs adapt to the changing weather. I want to adopt one of them.

The word *adapt* means to adjust to, or to make suitable. The word *adopt* means to choose or select.

Commonly Misused Words *(continued)*

Advice / Advise

I was asked to advise you. My advice to you is simple: RUN!

The verb *advise* means to give advice (guidance, helpful wisdom). The noun *advice* is the guidance or helpful wisdom given.

Affect / Effect

The medicine did not affect my cough. The medicine had several side effects.

The word *affect* means to influence. The word *effect*, as a noun, means result. As a verb, it means to accomplish.

All ready, Already

My sisters and I were all ready to go to the movie theater. Unfortunately, my brother was already there.

The adjective *all ready* means everyone is prepared. The adverb *already* is used to describe something that has happened previously.

Commonly Misused Words *(continued)*

All Right

This phrase has *two words*, and there are two *l*s in the first word. *Alright* is not correct.

Allusion / Delusion / Illusion

The man in the black cape gave the illusion that my penny turned into a quarter. Did you notice my allusion to a magician just now? He made me suffer the delusion that he could make me rich with his trick.

An *illusion* is something someone perceives to be real, but isn't. A *delusion* is something someone thinks is true, but isn't. An *allusion* is an indirect reference to someone or something someone said.

Among / Between

Dad divided the potato chips among his three sons. Mom divided the candy between her two daughters.

The word *among* should be used when describing more than two people or objects. The word *between* should be used when describing exactly two people or objects. There are exceptions to this rule; consult a grammar guide or ask your teacher for details.

Commonly Misused Words *(continued)*

Amount / Number

Can you guess the amount of money I have in my left pocket? Can you guess the number of coins I have in my right pocket?

The word *amount* is used when referring to the quantity of something, or to concepts or objects which are thought of as continuous. The word *number* is used when describing objects that are thought of as separate or distinct.

Anyway

There is no *s* at the end of the word. *Anyways* is not correct.

By / Buy

I will drive by the garage sale later today. I may buy a few things.

The word *by* means near or close to. The verb *buy* means to purchase.

Commonly Misused Words *(continued)*

Can / May

I can swim. May I swim in your pool?

The word *can* implies ability or capability. The word *may* is used when asking permission.

Capital / Capitol

Washington, D.C. is the capital of the United States. The Capitol is where the U.S. Congress works. Other cities have capitol buildings in their capitals too.

The word *capital* refers to the location of a state's or nation's government. This word is also used to refer to money or wealth, and is also the correct word when writing the phrase *capital letter*. The word *capitol* refers to the building in which government members meet.

Chose / Choose

Jenny chose her outfit for the first day of school. Tina still needs to choose hers.

The word *chose* is the past tense of the world *choose.*

Commonly Misused Words *(continued)*

Cite / Site

Juan needs to cite the Web sites he used in his report on train robberies. After that, he may visit the site of the town's old train station.

The verb *cite* means to refer to and credit a source when writing a research report. The noun *site* means a specific position or location, often of a town or building.

Climactic

The fireworks were a climactic finish to the July 4th celebration.

Note the *c* in the middle of the word. Without this middle *c*, the word would be *climatic*, which means relating to the climate (weather).

Compared to / Compared with

Ike compared the airplane to a bird. Sally compared the airplane with other modes of transportation.

Use *compared to* when indicating a resemblance or similarity. Use *compared with* when discussing similarities and differences.

Commonly Misused Words *(continued)*

Complement / Compliment

Mayra's blouse complemented her eyes. I gave her a compliment by telling her I liked her blouse.

A *complement* is something that completes or matches well with something else. A *compliment* is the giving of praise.

Confidant / Confident

Of course I told Mary; she is my confidant. I am confident that she did not tell anyone else.

The noun *confidant* means close, trusted friend. The adjective *confident* means to be sure or without doubt.

Could have, Would have

Note that these phrases use the word *have*, not *of*. The phrases *could of* and *would of* are not correct.

Different from

The phrase *different from* is correct. The phrase *different than* is not correct.

Commonly Misused Words *(continued)*

Dual / Duel

Mack had a dual-action flame thrower. He was ready for his duel with Ignacio.

Use the adjective *dual* when describing something that comes in pairs or twos. The noun *duel* means a formal fight or contest, usually with guns or swords.

Elicit / Illicit

Mrs. Johnson tried to elicit a response from Billy. She wanted him to describe his illicit activities.

The word *elicit* is a verb which means to bring forward or to draw out. The word *illicit* is an adjective which means illegal.

Emigrate from / Immigrate to

Juan emigrated from Mexico to the United States. He immigrated to the United States from Mexico.

The word *emigrate* means to leave. The word *immigrate* means to come to or come into.

Commonly Misused Words *(continued)*

Eminent / Imminent

The king is the most eminent man in all the land. His murder is imminent.

The adjective *eminent* (with only one *m*) means famous or important. The adjective *imminent* (with two *m*s) means about to happen soon.

Farther / Further

My dad wants to drive farther after dinner. This will further aggravate my mother.

The word *farther* indicates physical distance. The word *further* is used in all other cases, and indicates degree or extent.

Fewer / Less

I have fewer coins than you do, but you have less money.

The adjective *fewer* is used when referring to people or objects that are thought of as separate or distinct. The adjective *less* is used when referring to concepts which are thought of as continuous or "as a whole."

Commonly Misused Words *(continued)*

Good / Well

Sarah is a good girl. This pizza is not very good. Jeremy plays basketball well. How well can you play?

The word *well* is an adverb ("well done," "plays well with others") and an adjective ("I am well"). The word *good* is an adjective ("a good story") or a noun ("the greater good"). Don't use *good* as an adverb ("he writes good").

Hanged / Hung

The murderer was hanged in the center of town.
A plaque was hung to commemorate the fateful day.

The word *hanged* is used only when describing a person who is executed by hanging. The word *hung* should be used as the past tense of *hang* in all other cases.

Commonly Misused Words *(continued)*

Hardly / Barely / Scarcely

Jean could hardly (barely, scarcely) contain her excitement.

Do not put the word *not* in front of these words. *Jean could* not *hardly (barely, scarcely) contain her excitement* is not correct.

I.e. / E.g.

My mom is a stay-at-home mom, i.e., she's a chauffer.
I like snacks. E.g., candy bars, lollipops, and popcorn.

The abbreviation *i.e.* means *in other words*. The abbreviation *e.g.* means *for example*. Note that since *e.g.* indicates a partial list, it is redundant to add *etc.* at the end of a list introduced by this abbreviation.

Imply / Infer

The look on her face implied she was angry.
I inferred that she was angry from her scowl.

A speaker or actor *implies* by what she says and does. A listener or viewer *infers* by what was said and done.

Commonly Misused Words *(continued)*

Its / It's

A cat licks its fur to clean itself. That may be, but I think it's gross.

Its, without an apostrophe, should be used when some it possesses something. The word *its* is like the words *his* and *hers*, but is used when referring to an object or animal. *It's*, with the apostrophe, is the contraction for *it is*.

Kind of, Sort of, Type of, Variety of

Do not follow these phrases with the word *a*.
These are correct:
    It was some kind of dog.
    She caught some sort of virus.
These are not correct:
    It looks like a type of a rocket.
    She picked a variety of a pear.

Commonly Misused Words *(continued)*

Lead / Led

Joe was going to lead the way into the sewer, but Mary led the way instead. In the darkness, Mary bonked her head on a large lead pipe.

The verb *lead* (rhymes with *bead*) means to go first and show the way. The past tense of this verb is *led* (rhymes with *red*). When pronounced to rhyme with *led*, the word *lead* is a heavy, relatively soft, bluish-gray metal.

Commonly Misused Words *(continued)*

Lie, Lay, Lain / Lay, Laid / Lie, Lied

Present tense: I lie down on my bed to rest.
Past tense: Yesterday, I lay on my bed, thinking.
Past participle: I had lain there all morning.

Present tense: I lay my pencils on the desk.
Past tense: Yesterday, I laid my erasers on the desk.
Past participle: I had laid them there ever day this week.

I cannot tell a lie: I took the last piece of pie.
I lied to my mother about my homework.

The verb *lie*, which cannot take an object, means to recline, and *lie*, *lay*, and *lain* are the various forms of this word. The word *lay* means to put down, and *lay*, *laid*, and (have) *laid* are the various forms of this word. The verb *lie* also means to tell an untruth, and the word *lied* is the past tense of this verb.

Commonly Misused Words *(continued)*

Lose / Loose / Losing

My tennis shoes are loose. I think that's why we are losing the game. I am afraid we are going to lose.

The adjective *loose* is the opposite of tight. The verb *lose* is the opposite of win. Someone is *losing* if he or she is behind in a race or in the score.

Principal / Principle

Mrs. Johnson is the principal of our school. She taught us the principle that you should treat others the way you want to be treated.

The noun *principal* refers to the leader of a school. The noun *principle* means a general guideline or basic truth.

Precede / Proceed

Ivan preceded Juan in line. Both boys proceeded to walk to the lunchroom when told to do so.

The verb *precede* means to go before or in front of someone or something else. The verb *proceed* means to go forward in performing an action.

Commonly Misused Words *(continued)*

Quiet / Quit / Quite

Please be quiet. I really need you to quit making so much noise. You really are being quite annoying.

When used as an adjective, the word *quiet* means the opposite of loud. When used as a noun, the word *quiet* means an overall absence of loud sounds. The verb *quit* means to give up, to stop trying. The adjective *quite* means either (a) completely, wholly, or entirely ("not quite finished"); (b) actually, really, or truly ("quite a scare"); or (c) to a considerable extent or degree ("quite large").

Sat / Set / Sit

The cat sat on the mat. I set my newspaper down to watch her. Hopefully, she'll sit on my lap soon.

The verb *sit* means to rest upon with one's rear end. The past tense of this word is the word *sat*. The verb *set* means to place an object (or person) down on something (or someone).

Commonly Misused Words *(continued)*

Stationary / Stationery

The stationary guard stood watch all night. In the morning, I wrote him a letter on my new stationery.

The adjective *stationary* means standing still, or remaining in one place. The noun *stationery* is paper used for writing letters or notes.

Supposed to

Note the *d* at the end of the word. *Suppose to* is not correct. Hint: the phrase is past tense, which is why it has the *d* at the end of the first word.

Than / Then

I like pizza more than I like spinach. I'll eat my pizza, and then I'll go out and play baseball.

The word *than* refers to the comparison of two items. The word *then* relates to time and the ordering of events.

Commonly Misused Words *(continued)*

Their / There / They're

The neighbors should move their boat. Large vehicles are not allowed there. They're not being considerate.

The word *their* is a possessive pronoun used when describing the objects possessed by a collection of people. The word *there* has to do with location. The word *they're* is the contraction for *they are*.

Though / Through / Thorough / Throw, Threw

I liked the movie even though it was long. My mom snored through the whole thing. It was a thorough report on penguins. I like to throw a football around with my brother. My brother threw popcorn at the screen.

The word *though* means in spite of the fact that or although ("even though she tried very hard..."). The word *through* has to do with completing something. ("He walked through the door"). The adjective *thorough* means complete. The verb *throw* means to hurl with your arm, and *threw* is the past tense of this word.

Commonly Misused Words *(continued)*

To / Too / Two

I am going to the store. Mary is coming too. We'll buy two bottles of soda.

The word *to* means toward or in the direction of. The word *too* signifies that someone is joining one or more other people in doing something. The word *two* is the number that comes after one and before three.

Toward

There is no *s* at the end of the word. *Towards* is not correct.

Used to

Note the *d* at the end of the word. *Use to* is not correct. Hint: the phrase is past tense, which is why it has the *d* at the end of the first word.

Commonly Misused Words *(continued)*

Weather / Whether

Jay wanted to go to the beach because of the nice weather. I like to go to the beach whether it is hot or not.

The noun *weather* refers to the temperature, rain, snow, the wind, etc. The word *whether* is used to introduce the first of two or more alternatives.

Were / We're / Where / Wear

Where are you going for summer vacation? We're going to the beach. We were going to go to the beach, too. Be sure to wear lots of sunscreen if you decide to come.

The word *where* has to do with location or position. The word *we're* is a contraction for *we are*. The word *were* is the past tense of the word *are*. The verb *wear* has to do with clothing (as in wearing clothes, or wearing sunscreen) or with the deterioration of something ("using the brakes so much will wear down the brake pads").

Commonly Misused Words *(continued)*

Whose / Who's

Whose jacket is this? Who's going to the park with me?

The word *whose* is the possessive form of the word *who*. The word *who's* is the contraction for *who is* or *who has*.

Who / Which / That

That's the boy who hit me. My father didn't know which job to take. That's the car that I want.

Use *who* when referring to people or animals, robots, or monsters treated as people. Use *that* when referring to an object. Use *which* when referring to things or animals, not people.

Commonly Misused Words *(continued)*

Who / Whom / Whoever / Whomever

Who is in charge here? The teachers, two of whom are asleep, are in charge. Mr. Smythe is the teacher who is snoring in the corner. To whom can we turn for help? I say we should ask that teacher, whoever she is.

The words *who* and *whoever* are pronouns that are used as the subject of a verb. The words *whom* and *whomever* are pronouns that are used as the object of a verb.

Hint #1: Substitute *he/him* or *she/her*: If it's either *he* or *she*, then it's *who*; if it's *him* or *her*, then it's *whom*.

Hint #2: Every verb with a tense in a sentence must have a subject, which means using *who*.

Witch / Which

The witch had a long nose, a wart, and a scary cackle. Which of her potions did she use?

A *witch* has magical powers. The word *which* is used when indicating a selection between two or more objects, people, or situations.

Commonly Misused Words *(continued)*

Your / You're

I don't like <u>your</u> attitude. <u>You're</u> the one who started the fight.

The word *your* is the possessive form of the word *you*. The word *you're* is the contraction for *you are*.

Citing Sources

Here are the formatting rules* for the most common kinds of bibliographic entries. Pay close attention to the order of the included information as well as the punctuation between elements.

Remember:

- » Alphabetize by the author's last name.
- » If there's no author, alphabetize by title.
- » Always indent the second or third lines 5 spaces.
- » Leave 1 space after commas and 2 spaces after periods and colons.

* Modern Language Association (MLA) guidelines
Note: Use any guidelines provided by your teacher, especially if they differ from the following.

Web Site

Format: Author last name, First name (if given). "Title of article or page." Sponsor of Web site. Date of article. Web site address (URL).

Example: Smith, Chris. "Electronic Circuits." Circuits R Us. June 2007. http://www.something.com/evenmore.html.

(continued on next page)

Citing Sources *(continued)*

Book—Single Author

Format: Author last name, First name. Title of book. Place of publication: Publisher, Year of publication.

Example: Smith, Chris. The Magic of Electronic Circuits. Chicago: McGraw Hill, 2006.

Book—Two Authors

Format: First author last name, First name and Second author first and last name. Title of book. Place of publication: Publisher, Year of publication.

Example: Cline, Eric H. and Jill Rubalcaba. The Ancient Egyptian World. New York: Oxford University Press, 2005.

Book—No Author

Format: Title of book. Place of publication: Publisher, Year of publication.

Example: The World of Learning. London: Europa Publications, 1995.

(continued on next page)

Citing Sources *(continued)*

Encyclopedia (Print or CD-ROM)

Format: Author (if given) last name, First name. "Title of article." Title of encyclopedia. Year published. Volume number, Page number(s).

Example: "Electronics." Colliers Encyclopedia. 1998. Volume 5, 452-455.

Magazine Article

Format: Author last name, First name. "Title of article." Title of magazine. Date of magazine: Article page number(s).

Example: Smith, Chris. "Fun with Electronic Circuits." Electronics for Hobbyists. Mar. 2006: 21-27.

Onomatopoeia Words

Onomatopoeia is a word or a grouping of words that imitates the sound it is describing. Sometimes, using these words can give your writing an extra *oomph*, some *zing*, even make it go *bam*!

Here is a list of onomatopoeia words:

aack
ah
arf
baa
bam
bang
bark
beep
bing
bleep
blip
boing
boom
bowwow
buzz
cheep
chirp
choo-choo
chug
clack
clang
clank
clatter
click
clink
clip-clop
clomp
cluck
clunk
cock-a-doodle-do
cool
cough
crack
crackle
crash
creak
crunch
ding-a-ling
ding-dong
drip
eek
flap
grind
growl
grunt
ha-ha
hee-haw
hiss
hmmm
honk
hoot
howl
hum
kerchoo
kerplop
kerplunk
meow
moo
neigh
oink
ooh
oomph
ping

(continued on next page)

Onomatopoeia Words *(continued)*

plop
plunk
pong
pop
puff
purr
ring
roar
rip
ruff
rumble
rustle
screech
scrunch
sizzle
slop
slurp
smack
smash
snap
snort
splash
splat
sputter
squeak
squeal
squish
swish
tap
tee-hee
thud
thump
tick
tick-tock
tinkle
twang
tweet
ugh
uh-huh
waa
whack
whee
whirr
whiz
whomp
whoop
zing
zip
zoom

Story Elements

Characters

Characters are the people (or perhaps animals, aliens, or robots) in your story. Major characters are those few who are the most important. Minor characters are all the rest.

» **Make your characters believable.**

Your characters should do and say things that your readers believe they would do and say.

» **Make your characters interesting.**

Major characters should be interesting and multi-faceted, not "cardboard cutouts" that never change. Minor characters help move your story along, but don't need to be as completely described.

» **Major characters should learn and change.**

» **Your hero should (normally) be likable.**

» **Your villain should be powerful.**

Your antagonist(s) (or villains) should be as powerful as—or more powerful than—your protagonist; your hero's job shouldn't be easy.

(continued on next page)

Story Elements *(continued)*

Plot

Plot is the series of events that take place in your story. It's the action, or what happens, in your story.

» **Events should be related by cause-and-effect.**

Events should not seem to be random or unrelated. Describe or imply the connections between events so they feel related and connected.

» **Have a beginning, middle, and end.**

Stories should have a beginning, middle, and end. In the beginning, you should introduce most if not all of your characters, and show things as they "normally are." In the middle, conflicts occur and complications are overcome. Finally, in the end, your story is wrapped up, usually with your hero(s) "winning" or at least changed or having learned something.

» **Advance plot with dialogue.**

Normally, you move your plot forward by describing what happens (this is called exposition). You can—and should—also advance plot within your dialogue.

(continued on next page)

Story Elements *(continued)*

Conflict

Conflict is the tension between and within your characters. It usually comes from the clash between two or more characters' goals, and is what makes you upset, angry, or worried when you read a story.

Conflict does not have to be physical (such as a fight); it can take the form of challenges that have to be overcome or disagreements between characters.

» **Conflict is what makes stories interesting.**
Stories are usually boring without it.

» **Conflict rises then falls.**
Conflict in your story should rise, getting progressively more tense, until the climax of your story. After the climax, conflict should fall away quickly.

» **Two types of conflict: internal and external.**
External conflict is conflict between your character(s) and something in the physical world, such as other characters, obstacles, or the weather.

Internal conflict occurs within the mind of a character. Examples of internal conflict include overcoming fear and overcoming or changing personality traits.

(continued on next page)

Story Elements *(continued)*

Setting

Setting is the environment in which the action takes place. It usually includes time period and location.

- **Use setting to avoid confusion.**

  Tell your readers where and when things are happening so they aren't confused. Describe using all five senses, not just sight.

- **Describe what your characters hear, feel, smell, and taste as well as what they see.**

  Sensory details—sights, textures, sounds, smells, and flavors—help your readers see, feel, hear, smell, or taste what you are describing, making them feel like they are "right there" in your story world.

- **Setting affects mood.**

  Even with the same characters speaking the same dialogue and performing the same actions, a scene set at midnight in a dark alley will feel different than a scene set on a sunny spring day in a park.

- **Match objects, language, time**

  The objects (props, tools, etc.) and language used by your characters must match the time and place of your story.

(continued on next page)

Story Elements *(continued)*

Mood

Mood is the atmosphere of a story created by the story's setting and its characters and their actions. It refers to how the reader emotionally responds to these elements—sadness, happiness, anger, etc. Setting, images, details, and words all contribute to creating a story's mood.

» **Description choice affects mood.**

Choose the way you describe things (settings, characters, etc.) in order to set the mood you want for your story.

» **Be consistent.**

The mood you set—through detailed descriptions of your setting(s) and characters—needs to be consistent with the storyline and your story's resolution. Don't make everything in your story dark and sinister and then have everything suddenly come out happy and bright, or vice versa.

(continued on next page)

Story Elements *(continued)*

Dialogue

Dialogue is what your characters say. It appears within quotation marks.

» **Avoid pointless dialogue.**

Dialogue should advance the plot or help readers understand your characters.

Real conversations between real people are usually boring, repetitive, and full of time-eating *um*s and *ah*s. Any dialogue you write for your characters should be better than this! Cut words and phrases that don't move the plot forward, explain or advance your characters, or both.

» **No speeches.**

Don't let a character talk for too long at one time. Readers usually find this boring.

A good rule is that you should usually have no more than three or four lines of dialogue by one character before someone else speaks, or before somebody performs some action.

» **Break up long stretches of dialogue with action.**

(continued on next page)

Story Elements *(continued)*

Point of View

Point of view (POV) is the position of the narrator in relation to a story. It can be first-person (a character in the story), third-person (an outsider who sees into the mind of one of the characters), or omniscient (an all-knowing outsider).

» **First person is personal but limited.**

First person POV gives the most personal connection to your story, but if you use it, you can't describe anything anyone else is thinking, or anything that happens when your point of view character is not in a scene.

» **Omniscient is powerful but less close.**

Omniscient POV allows you to describe what any character is thinking and what all characters are doing, but usually feels the least personal to your readers.

» **Third person is like first but using *she* or *he*, not *I*.**

Third person POV is slightly less personal than first person POV.

(continued on next page)

Story Elements *(continued)*

Tone

Tone is the attitude (stated or implied) a writer has toward her subject. Your tone might be optimistic, pessimistic, serious, humorous, bitter, etc. Tone is communicated through diction, style, and any opinion(s) you express.

» **Tone affects readers' feelings about your story and your characters.**

» **Match tone to POV character.**

If using first person POV, your tone must match the personality and attitudes of your POV character.

If using third person POV or omniscient POV, you can use your own tone, even if it is different than the character(s) you are describing.

Literary Terms

alliteration Repeated consonant sounds occurring at the beginning of words or within words. Example: Rascally rabbits rarely relax.

antagonist The character or force that opposes the protagonist.

climax The result of the crisis. The high point of the story for the reader; involves the highest interest and greatest emotion. The point at which the outcome can be predicted.

conflict The clash between opposing forces. The essence of fiction; creates plot. Usually identified as one of four kinds: Man versus... Man, Nature, Society, or Self

crisis The point at which the conflict between opposing forces becomes most intense. Occurs before or at the same time as the climax.

dynamic character A character who changes as a result of what happens to him or her.

(continued on next page)

Literary Terms *(continued)*

epic An extended narrative poem recounting actions, travels, adventures, and heroic episodes. Examples: Homer's *Iliad* and *Odyssey*.

euphemism The substitution of a mild or less negative word or phrase for a harsh, blunt one. Example: calling someone "frugal" rather than "cheap."

exposition The introductory material which gives the setting, creates the tone, presents the characters, and presents other facts necessary to understanding the story.

falling action The events after the climax which close a story.

figurative language Describing something by comparing it with something else. Examples: similes and metaphors.

flashback The presentation of events that happened before the time of the current narration or the current events in the story.

(continued on next page)

Literary Terms *(continued)*

foil	A character who provides a contrast to the protagonist.
foreshadowing	The use of hints or clues to suggest what will happen later in thc story.
hyperbole	An exaggerated statement used to heighten effect. Example: "I've reminded you to take out the trash 10 billion times!"
inciting force	The event or character that triggers conflict.
irony	The contrast between what is expected or what appears to be and what actually is.
major characters	The significant characters in a story. Almost always three-dimensional, they have flaws as well as good qualities. Their goals and/or values change.

(continued on next page)

Literary Terms *(continued)*

metaphor	A figure of speech which involves an implied comparison between two unlike things. Example: Emily was a vault, never revealing her secrets.
meter	The rhythmic pattern produced when words are arranged so that their stressed and unstressed syllables fall into a more or less regular sequence, resulting in repeated patterns of accent.
minor characters	Supporting characters in a story. Almost always flat or two-dimensional, they have few striking qualities and are usually all good or all bad. Sometimes referred to as "static" as they rarely change as a result of the events of a story.
mood	The feeling or atmosphere of a story. Setting, images, details, and words all contribute to creating a story's mood.

(continued on next page)

Literary Terms *(continued)*

onomatopoeia The use of words that mimic sounds. Examples: buzz, chirp, hiss.

oxymoron A figure of speech that combines two contradictory terms. Examples: jumbo shrimp, good grief, friendly competition.

palindrome A word or phrase that can be read the same backwards or forwards. Examples: eye, mom, pop, level, poop.

personification A figure of speech which gives the qualities of a person to an animal, an object, or an idea. Examples: talking animals, Father Time, a smiling moon, robots with emotions

plot The set of events that take place in a story. It is the action, or what happens, in a story.

(continued on next page)

Literary Terms *(continued)*

point of view (persona)	The position of the narrator in relation to the story. Can be first-person (a character in the story), third-person (an outsider who sees into the mind of one of the characters), or omniscient (an all-knowing outsider).
protagonist	The main character of a story.
resolution	Also knows as *denouement.* Concludes the action. The final resolution of the plot.
rhyme	The similarity between syllable sounds at the end of two or more lines.
rising action	A series of events that builds from the conflict in a story. Begins with the inciting force and ends with the climax.
setting	The environment for the action of a fictional work. It can include time period, place, and mood, and is enhanced by description using the senses: sight, taste, touch, sight, smell, and sound.

(continued on next page)

Literary Terms *(continued)*

simile — A figure of speech which involves comparing two unlike things using the word *like* or *as*. Example: Her golden hair was like shimmering rays of sunlight.

symbolism — The use of a person, place or object which has a meaning in itself but represents other meanings as well. Example: the ticking of a clock to emphasize a person running out of time.

theme — The main idea or underlying meaning of a literary work.

tone — The author's attitude, stated or implied, toward a subject. Includes attitudes such as optimism, pessimism, seriousness, humorous, bitterness, etc.

Quotation Marks

Direct Quotations:

You use quotation marks to show words exactly as written or spoken by someone.

> "I feel hungry," she said.

You do not need quote marks if you are merely stating information that was spoken.

> She said that she felt hungry. (No quotes!)

Splitting Quotations:

Remember to use two sets of quotation marks when a quotation is split apart.

> "Life is full of challenges," said Grandmother, "and they all make us stronger."

Partial Quotations:

You need to use quotation marks even if you are only using part of the words stated or written by someone. If you are starting in the middle of a statement, you should begin with a lower case letter instead of a capital letter.

> In the article, the expert agreed that "ignoring global warming will have devastating consequences."

Quotation Marks *(continued)*

Quotation Marks for Titles:

You use quotation marks to indicate a title for magazine articles, short stories, essay, poems, songs and other short works.

> Have you read the short story "Riding the Bullet" by Steven King?

> My favorite poem is "The Tell Tale Heart" by Edgar Allen Poe.

Quotations within Quotations:

Use single quote marks at the beginning and ending of a title or a quotation within a direct quote.

> "I've just read 'The Tell Tale Heart'," said Tom.

> Mary said, "When I answered the question in class, Mrs. Reynolds said, 'Great job, Mary!'"

Dialogue Tags (Instead of Said, Etc.)

When choosing dialogue tags it is important to remember that *said* is perfectly acceptable. The tags below will provide variety, but remember to use them sparingly. **The words and emotions in your dialogue are much more important than the dialog tags you choose.**

<u>"Simply" said:</u>

added
admitted
agreed
announced
answered
began
called
continued
explained
remarked
repeated
replied
responded

<u>"Emotionally" said:</u>

begged
blurted
choked
cried
declared
demanded
exclaimed
gasped
gulped
gushed
implored
insisted
persisted
pleaded
proclaimed
protested
shouted
shrieked

(continued on next page)

Dialogue Tags *(continued)*

"Humorously" said:

chuckled	guffawed	joked
grinned	hooted	laughed

"Negatively" said:

babbled	growled	rambled
barked	grumbled	roared
blubbered	hissed	scoffed
blustered	howled	screamed
cackled	mimicked	screeched
chattered	moaned	taunted
complained	mocked	teased
droned	pestered	whined
fumed	pouted	yelled

"Softly" said:

breathed	mumbled	whispered
hinted	muttered	
mouthed	sighed	

"Asked" not said:

asked	pondered	questioned
inquired	queried	

Sentence Starters

Here is a list of ways to begin your sentences. These are particularly useful for expository writing.

To introduce your topic:

Are you aware that...
Did you know that...
Do you remember when...
Have you ever thought about...
It is fascinating to learn about...
Let's take a look at...
There are many reasons why...
Try to visualize...
Would you believe that...
You may be surprised to learn that...

To introduce surprising or unusual thoughts or facts:

Actually,...
Amazingly,...
Astonishingly,...
Do you realize that...
Have you ever thought about...
Have you ever wondered...
Imagine...
Incredibly,...
Interestingly enough,...
It is amazing to think about...
It is hard to believe, but...
Strangely enough,...
Surprisingly,...
Very few people know that...

(continued on next page)

Sentence Starters *(continued)*

To introduce universal (or commonly-known) thoughts, facts, or points of view:
Certainly,...
Experience shows that...
Experts agree that...
Frequently,...
Generally,...
Granted,...
Historically,...
In fact,...
In general,...
In most cases...
It is true that...
Most people agree that...
Most people believe that...
Most people would argue that...
Naturally,...
Normally,...
Of course,...
Often times,...
Sometimes,...
Surely,...
Typically,...
Undoubtedly,...
Usually,...
Without a doubt...
You will find that...

(continued on next page)

Sentence Starters *(continued)*

To show cause and effect:
As a result,...
Because of...
Consequently,...
For this/that reason,...
It follows that...
So,...
The result is...
Therefore,...
Thus,...

To add information:
Additionally,...
Also,...
An example of this would be...
For example,...
For instance,...
Furthermore,...
In addition,...
Moreover,...
To illustrate,...

To summarize or conclude:
Finally,...
In conclusion,...
In summary,...
Lastly,...
To conclude,...
To summarize,...

Proofreader's Marks

¶	begin a new paragraph
∧	insert specified letters, words, or sentences
∧ ,	insert a comma
“ ∨ ” ∨	insert quotation marks
⊙	insert period
’ ∨	insert an apostrophe
	take out words, sentences, and punctuation marks
/	change an uppercase letter to lowercase
≡	change a lowercase letter to uppercase
	transpose; reverse letters or words
#	insert a space
sp	spelling is incorrect
(sp)	spell out word
	close the space

Proofreader's Marks—Example

My Summer Vacation

My family and I had a fantastic summer vacation. We spent the entire Summer in England. We visited many historical landmarks.

In London, we visited Bucking ham Palace. It is the officialresidence in London of the Queen of England. We watched the changing of the guard, and I remember my youngest sister, Sally, saying, How do they keep from smiling? After visiting Buckingham Palace, we went to the Tower of London and saw the the Crown Jewels. We saw also the worlds largest Feris wheel The Eye. On the last day of the trip, we went to Trafalgar Sq. and did some shopping. I highly recommend everyone visit England. It is an amazing country. I liked it so much I asked my parents if we could go again next year.